Courage to Tri

To my husband John who faithfully supports all my #trycourage endeavors and to Bailey, who joyfully swim, bikes, and runs faster than me. To Sadie, my favorite running partner for 13 years: I miss you, I love you always, and I hope you're running free in heaven.

Bethany Rutledge

FINISH YOUR
FIRST TRIATHLON.

A MOTIVATIONAL
HOW-TO FOR WOMEN.

Meyer & Meyer Sport

British Library Cataloguing in Publication Data
A catalogue record for this book is available from the British Library

Courage to Tri
Maidenhead: Meyer & Meyer Sport (UK) Ltd., 2018
ISBN: 978-1-78255-135-5

© 2018 by Meyer & Meyer Sport (UK) Ltd.
Aachen, Auckland, Beirut, Cairo, Cape Town, Dubai, Hägendorf, Hong Kong, Indianapolis,
Manila, New Delhi, Singapore, Sydney, Tehran, Vienna

Member of the World Sports Publishers' Association (WSPA), www.w-s-p-a.org
Printed by C-M Books, Ann Arbor, MI, USA
ISBN: 978-1-78255-135-5
Email: info@m-m-sports.com
www.m-m-sports.com

CONTENTS

Preface 9

Foreword 11

Acknowledgments 13

Introduction 15

Part One Get Inspired 19

Chapter 1 Busting Myths 21

Chapter 2 Finding Your Why 29

Chapter 3 How Tri Can Change You 40

Chapter 4 Overcoming Obstacles 50

Chapter 5 Moms Who Tri 70

Chapter 6 Finding Accountability and Community 78

Chapter 7 Common Concerns 90

Chapter 8 Triathlon and Body Image 98

Part Two Get Prepped 113

Chapter 9 Get Geared Up 114

Chapter 10 Races and Coaches 125

Chapter 11 Making Space to Train 139

Chapter 12 Preparation Goals 152

Part Three Get Trained 163

Chapter 13 Training Pep Talk 164

Chapter 14 Training Plan Basics 170

Chapter 15 Swim Training 189

Chapter 16 Cycling Training 203

Chapter 17 Run Training.................................. 222

Chapter 18 Transition Training.......................... 233

Chapter 19 Tackling Nutrition........................... 243

Part Four Get Set.. 253

Chapter 20 Your First Race 256

Chapter 21 After the Race................................ 270

Appendix 274

PREFACE

Have you dreamed of crossing a finish line but have no idea how to get from now to the starting line? Do you have a secret goal you're terrified to tackle? Whether it's a 5K, triathlon, or another starting line, we'll provide the inspiration and insight to tackle your first race with confidence.

You *are* good enough, you are athletic enough, and now is as good a time as any. I'm inviting you, personally, to join me on a journey to your first triathlon.

> *"If you can run or walk a mile, then you can train to complete a sprint triathlon."* – Jim Boylan, Atlanta Tri Club Founder

It may sound cliché, but these are words to live by. Even as a brand new athlete, completing a triathlon is within your reach, *if* you put in the effort to "try."

In these pages, you'll get inspired by women just like you who found confidence, overcame unhealthy lifestyles, and made new friends along the way.

Whether you're 12 or 85; a student, executive, or stay-at-home mom; fit or a self-proclaimed couch potato, learn how to complete a triathlon with just a few months of effort and dedication.

» Part One: Get Inspired—Find a powerful driving "why."

» Part Two: Get Prepped—Prepare to achieve your finish line dreams.

» Part Three: Get Trained—Learn the basics of swim, bike, and run.

» Part Four: Get Set—Explore every step on race day.

Two added bonuses:

» #TriCourage—stories from everyday women who overcame obstacles and changed their lives.

» #TriLessons—anecdotes from others who balanced triathlon with real life.

FOREWORD

Advertised as "one of the toughest races in America," the Hogpen Hill Climb rises nearly 3000 feet in the North Georgia Mountains. Run every January, the typically miserable weather conditions perfectly complement the 18 kilometers of leg- and lung-burning terrain. Hogpen might not sound like a place one goes to make friends, but it's where I first met Bethany Rutledge.

Bethany and her Atlanta Triathlon Club crew were regulars at races like Hogpen during the decade I called Atlanta home. Whether it was the "toughest race in America," a competitive local triathlon, or a favorite all-women's 5K, if a starting line was involved, I expected to see Bethany. Clad in the black and red of ATC, she was typically surrounded by other athletes of all shapes, sizes, and age ranges. Many were obviously race veterans, others inquisitive beginners, and Bethany seemed to have encouraging words for all of them, while simultaneously maintaining her own race focus and often earning herself a spot on the podium.

I've been lucky to follow Bethany's triathlon journey as a fellow competitor, often running the same race course and sharing post-race laughs and stories over chicken soup or orange slices. Now, you, too, can be a part of those finish line festivities. In *The Courage to Tri,* Bethany welcomes all women to put on a pair of running shoes and join the club. Learn from Bethany and other women who share stories of triumph and transformation as they navigate their way through the endurance sports world.

We were all once beginners, we've all had help along the way, and now, thanks to Bethany, we want to do our part to pay it forward. I hope you find your own Hogpen Hill Climb, your own mountaintop finish, an accomplishment that makes you proud of yourself, and a place where you're greeted by friends, eager to hear the story of your day. There's always room for more women on the starting line and always a place at the post-race refreshment table for those who have the *courage to tri*.

–Haley Chura
Ironman and 70.3 Champion, triathlon coach, and co-host of the "Ironwomen" podcast

ACKNOWLEDGMENTS

Thanks to my all-time favorite training partners: Sadie, Bailey, and John. Thank you to John Rutledge for supporting my dreams in triathlon, writing, and beyond. Thanks to my dad who instilled my love of running. And thanks to my mom who taught me to be independent and self-sufficient. Thanks to my in-laws Ken and Sherrie Rutledge who have been amazing cheerleaders along the way.

Thanks to the members of Atlanta Tri Club and Energy Lab who are not only training partners, but a family, and John and I appreciate the chance to "do life" with this wonderful group. Thanks to all the amazing athletes I've had the pleasure of coaching. Hopefully I taught you all a thing or two; you've taught me too many life lessons to count.

Thanks to all my favorite training partners over the years. Some of my fondest memories are long, meandering bike rides, ending up at a gas station in the middle of nowhere not sure how we got there, or how we'll get home, but happy nonetheless. Thanks to the best spectacheerers I know, Michelle Crossman and Sondra Choung, who've turned many a rural race into a five-star vacation complete with themed costumes and a five-part tracking strategy.

Thank you to everyone who contributed to this book in some way. I ran out of space long before I ran out of wonderful women to feature.

» Thanks to my beta readers and content editors: Amy Hafner, Angela Nelms, Kathryn Taylor, Kim Janke, Lillian Pettit, Marilia Brocchetto, and Sara Scott.

» Thanks to everyone who provided a story or quote. I received so many great ones, I couldn't fit them all. Thank you to Haley Chura, Sybil Jacobson, Debbie Wells, Dani Grabol, Kat Gurd, Marilia Brocchetto, Allie Bachelder, Kathryn Taylor, Amy Hafner, Lindsay Waibel, Cori James, and Heather Reynolds.

» Thank you to those athletes who were willing to share their heart journeys in the pages of this book: Deirdre DeKock, Dusty Scott, Jenny Johnson, and Meg Geshay.

» Thanks to my subject matter experts: Abby Keenan, Jesica D'Avanza, Ilana Katz, Dr. Melissa Smith, Candace Doby, and Megan Melgaard.

» Thanks to the best critique group who gave valuable feedback even though they don't live and breathe triathlon: Heather Spitzberg, Erin Burba, and Kristen Stewart.

INTRODUCTION

John and me at our first 5K in Fayetteville, NC

MY FALSE START

I completed my first triathlon in 2009, but the idea was sparked years earlier during my then-current exercise routine—a tortuous out-and-back three-mile jog with a smoke break halfway. I'm not sure *how* I first thought of it; I was probably craving some fun. Because my "training" was pure drudgery, a punishment jog, a half-hearted attempt to burn a couple calories from the couple thousand extra I'd had the night before.

I was far from triathlon ready for a few reasons: I had little aerobic fitness, and I knew nothing about triathlon. I also lacked a driving *why*—a good enough reason to go for it—along with a when.

So instead of tri-ing, I just thought about it a lot and wondered whether I *could* do it, listing pluses and minuses from my experience. Swimming. Plus: I dog-paddled two miles across Lake Eloise on a dare after high school graduation; I signed up for a swimming class in college. Minus: I couldn't move my arms after the three-hour swim, and I dropped the swim class before the first day (I found out it met at 6 AM).

Cycling. Plus: I rode around the neighborhood for hours as a kid, and more recently, I borrowed my roommate's mountain bike. Minus: I was a kid a long time ago, *and* I was sore after riding one mile across campus.

And then there was running. I felt pretty good there; I ran races with my dad as a kid and on and off since. But, I didn't *enjoy* running, and I heard you can't listen to music during a tri, much less take a smoke break.

As far as the financial part of things, my sitch was *all* minus, literally and figuratively. My bank account balance was less-than-zero. I'd recently overdrafted writing a check for tacos at Acapulco—again—and I wasn't coming into a windfall anytime soon.

The verdict? I had limited technical ability in the sports, but not *zero*. Physically, I could probably do it, if I trained and dropped some bad habits. But mentally I was *so* far away. Yet, I felt certain I would do a triathlon *someday*. To remind myself of my dream, I bought the book *Your First Triathlon* and put it on my coffee table. I wouldn't think about triathlon again for years and never imagined that book and a three-mile jog—with a Parliament Light break—would lead to racing all over the world. But they did!

Part One
Get Inspired

In this section, we'll bust common myths about triathletes and discuss your reason for tri-ing.

Then we'll discuss common obstacles on your tri journey and how to overcome them.

By the end of this section, you should be inspired to start your training journey.

1

BUSTING MYTHS

Before my husband John and I attended our first tri club meeting, we had many preconceived notions about triathletes. Here's the gist: they would be overly tan, semi-pro athletes with less than 10% body fat who only cared about winning races. They'd be scornful of newbies like us, reluctant to give up any trade secrets. They might even *laugh* at our goal to do a sprint distance triathlon—or worse—tell us we were aiming too high. Silly, right? Yet because of those highly exaggerated fears, we almost skipped the meeting.

But I'm so glad we went. Because *none* of the above turned out to be true, and that meeting launched us on an exciting journey.

What do *you* think of when you hear the word triathlete? Here are a few common myths about triathletes, followed by the truth.

WHAT ARE SOME INCORRECT ASSUMPTIONS YOU MADE ABOUT TRIATHLETES?

» *"They are all intimidating and scary."* – Smitha

» *"They eat healthfully."* – Susie

» *"They're morning people"* – Matt

MYTH 1: TRIATHLETES SHOULD HAVE A BACKGROUND IN SWIM, BIKE, OR RUN.

"They can all swim. I prove that false." – Andrew

There is no "typical" triathlon background. Many triathletes have *no* background in swim, bike, or run, yet go on to complete events with success. Every Monday night at our tri club swim practice, swimmers in the "beginner lane" learn to swim, many from scratch. And, each tri season, we celebrate first finish lines with those same athletes.

Sondra came to triathlon with virtually no sporting background, learning to swim and bike only after committing to a race. Prior to age 35, she stuck exclusively to step aerobics for exercise. She never considered herself particularly athletic, either, yet a 5K led to a sprint triathlon and then the eventual completion of IRONMAN Augusta 70.3.

Of course, some triathletes *do* have a sporting background, like Debbie, a former collegiate swimmer turned sedentary adult. She discovered triathlon as an escape from a hated job and found greater fitness, athleticism, and new friends as a result.

The point is, even if you're starting from ground zero level fitness, you *can* complete a tri. We have a saying at the Atlanta Triathlon Club that is attributed to club founder Jim Boylan: "If you can run or walk a mile, then you can train to complete a sprint triathlon."

MYTH 2: TRIATHLONS ARE FOR YOUNG PEOPLE.

"'Just try it' is a fitting mantra as we get older and stuck in the familiar, often reluctant to do new things." – Sybil

Triathlon, like golf and tennis, is truly a lifelong sport. John and I discovered this when we attended my first half-iron distance race, Gulf Coast. There, we were amazed by the health and vitality of athletes in the older age groups. I enviously watched the 75 to 79 award winners jump on—and off—the podium blocks with ease after crushing the race (while I limped around at a snail's pace). Since then, athletes continue to defy age and redefine what's possible. Sibyl Jacobson, who hails from the 75 to 79 age group, finished her first triathlon at age 61 and recently won her age group at IRONMAN Chattanooga 70.3.

Many pro athletes hit their prime in their mid-thirties and race pro into their forties. And on the age group level, it's not uncommon for many of the fastest amateurs to be 45-plus.

MYTH 3: ALL TRIATHLETES RACE COMPETITIVELY.

"They are all rail-thin, super-fast, and out for blood." – Lauren

Many assume *all* triathletes have Type A personalities. While the sport attracts its fair share of intense, goal-oriented individuals, athletes enter the sport for many other reasons.

For example, Kathryn was searching for community after moving to a new town and found it in triathlon. Lindsay was working through the pain of a divorce and found new friends and self-confidence after she started running. And Laura, looking for a personal challenge, found a supportive community and a sport that made her feel "alive."

MYTH 4: TRIATHLETES ARE UNFRIENDLY.

"I figured they'd be very fit, extremely focused, and possibly even annoyed at the new girl with no clue." – Kathryn

I didn't expect to make friends at our first tri club meeting. In fact, I was surprised to be invited to a run and a bike ride. Weren't they afraid we'd slow them down? Weren't they worried we'd ask too many questions? Nearly all the triathletes I met were friendly, *even* after I admitted I'd never competed in the Olympics or played a D1 sport. (Turns out, they hadn't either!)

MYTH 5: TRIATHLETES ARE OBSESSED.

"Triathletes spend all their time training, thinking about training, or talking about training. They all race IRONMAN distance, and they've been racing their entire lives." – Bethany

Okay, some are that way. But not *all* triathletes spend their vacations racing and riding bikes every weekend. Some athletes race one or two times a month while others participate once per year.

There are triathletes who cross the finish line and then relegate their bike to the basement, and others who train and race for decades. There are also athletes who train and compete solely in short-course races (more on the distances later) and those who compete in IRONMAN (the one you've seen on TV).

ARE THERE MANY WOMEN IN TRIATHLON?

Some of my favorite ladies about to start the John Tanner Sprint Triathlon in 2016

According to 2015 statistics, women comprise 38% of USA Triathlon members, the sport's national governing body. The designation of triathlon as an NCAA Emerging Sport for Women promises to bring that percentage up higher. So far, twenty schools have added varsity triathlon to their program.

USA Triathlon has also driven women's triathlon participation with the recently launched WIN (Women's Initiative) program, supporting women's events, clinics, and women-only start waves around the country.

Women for Tri, the branded initiative funded by World Triathlon Corporation, has dispersed over $157,000 to tri clubs invested in increasing women's participation and collegiate programs.

GETTING STARTED RIGHT

Atlanta Tri Club coaches, 2018

Our first tri club meeting proved many of our initial assumptions were wrong. In some ways, triathletes were the *opposite* of what John and I had expected. There were all sizes, all ages, all levels, *and they were all triathletes.*

The meeting also demonstrated how little we knew about the sport. There were so many things to learn, and some of them couldn't be solved using Google. For this reason, we were advised to *avoid* buying a ton of gear until we learned more about the sport. But I was ready to jump in! Why shouldn't I rush to get all the equipment I'd eventually need anyway?

That was my rationale as I gave my wallet a workout the very next day. I found an ill-fitting road bike at Play It Again Sports, some closeout tri suits online, even a "lot" of shorts on eBay that should have been listed as underwear.

Fortunately, most of the mistakes—and yes, those purchases were *all* mistakes—were fixable. The bike was given a new home, the ill-fitting gear was donated, and I never wore those ridiculous "shorts" in public.

Those were just errors I made in the first two days of my triathlon "career." Always one to act before thinking, I learned many lessons the hard way. If I could go back in time, I would approach things in the right order. Fortunately, you have that chance. To truly get started right, your first step should be finding your "why."

Takeaway: Myths about triathletes can intimidate newbies interested in trying the sport. But nearly anyone can complete a triathlon. Approaching things in a systematic way will save you time and money later. The first step in your journey is finding your source of motivation.

TERMS TO KNOW

Sprint triathlon—A sprint isn't a standard distance and generally ranges from a 400- to 750-yard swim, a 10- to 18-mile bike, and a 2- to 4-mile run. It takes most athletes 1 to 2 hours to complete.

2

FINDING YOUR WHY

Why do you want to do a running race or triathlon? To look better? To feel better? Because your friends are doing it? What is *your* driving why? To figure it out, Certified Mental Performance Consultant Abby Keenan recommends listing your current motivations.

If you're unsure, examine your past motivations for participating in other sports or activities. I'll use myself as an example. In high school and college, I stuck with cheerleading and pole vaulting primarily for *social* reasons.

To illustrate, here's how a typical track practice went down: My childhood friend Chandra and I zoomed around campus in my red Saturn, practice poles sticking out the windows. Next, we stopped by Dunkin' Donuts for a Coffee Coolatta and a six-pack of donuts. After *all* that, we'd practice. Sometimes.

Beyond social reasons, my driving motivation for exercise was *calorie burn*. In high school, I was constantly trying to reduce weight so I could be a flyer (the person at the top of the stunt) instead of a backspot (the person who catches the person doing a stunt). Then, in college, I was endlessly battling the freshman fifteen, or, in my case, twenty.

What would Abby say about my past motivation? She would note my driving motives were external and recommend finding internal motivation based on personal choice and inherent enjoyment.

Abby describes internal motivation as "interest without consequences," like enjoyment of an activity or the satisfaction of meeting a goal. Intrinsic motivation allows for better focus with less distraction and leads to less stress when mistakes are made. Internal motivation leads to increased self-efficacy and confidence.

In comparison, extrinsic motivation includes material rewards or the approval of others. Athletes who are motivated extrinsically tend to focus more on performance or competition. Here are some examples of external motivation:

» You're motivated by getting a reward. For example, you race to get a really awesome finisher's medal.

» You're avoiding punishment. For instance, a physician tells you to lose weight or go on medication.

» You're motivated by shame. For example, you exercise to burn calories or because you hate the way you look.

» You're motivated by guilt. For example, you participate because you told a friend you would.

Some form of extrinsic motivation is always present, but it becomes a problem when the reward starts controlling your behavior. For example, you race because you feel like you *should* to meet the expectations of others. Too much extrinsic motivation can also erode your intrinsic motives. For example, if your goal was to win, and you didn't, you see the race as a waste.

Takeaway: What were some of your past motives for participating in sport? Were those reasons driven primarily by internal or external reasons?

FINDING AN INTERNAL WHY

It's hard to find internal motivation when you begin a new activity. But even if you're only motivated externally now, it doesn't mean that it will always be that way. For example, sticking to a routine can lead to satisfaction, which, in turn, provides energy to keep moving forward. Here's how finding internal motivation happened to me.

> *"We often set goals because we're externally motivated. While these aren't the best for sustaining motivation long term, they are often a good starting point!"* – Abby Keenan

In 2008, I was in a fitness rut. I was about to turn 27, which felt like a banner birthday, delineating official adulthood.

I was in the worst shape of my adult life. As a sales rep, my job included schlepping fried chicken and cupcakes to customers, sometimes multiple times a day. My daily exercise had dwindled to walking the dogs. My clothes were getting tight, and I cycled between the same three suits that—I thought—hid my weight gain best. With weight loss as the primary motive, I made an amorphous goal to "get in shape" by my birthday.

I needed something big and scary to motivate me, so John and I joined an outdoor bootcamp that consisted of daily push-ups, sit-ups, squats, and running. It was hard, but sticking to my goal and seeing improvement was exciting. After a few months I almost forgot my birthday goal and instead enjoyed the experience for its own sake. It was the first time I'd experienced intrinsic motivation in sport.

Next, John and I entered the Navy Seal Fitness Challenge. The event tested timed push-ups, pull-ups, sit-ups, a 1.5-mile run, and a 500-yard swim. I trained obsessively for weeks, and "race day" was so exciting. I remember my exact run time, swim time, and pull-up numbers in the way only runners and triathletes can conjure up their PRs decades after the event.

Completing a challenge, especially one I wasn't sure I could accomplish, triggered something. I experienced immense satisfaction from setting a goal and then meeting it. It was addictive, and I wanted more.

Takeaway: Even if new activities are initiated for extrinsic reasons, intrinsic motives have longer staying power and can come later.

FINDING YOUR CURRENT WHY

What is your current why? You may have several. Pull out a piece of paper and write them down or scribble them in the margin of this book.

There are different categories of whys. First, there's the why that sounds noble, the one you tell your mom about. "I want to keep my heart healthy," or "I want to show others they can do it, too."

Then there are the whys that belong on a t-shirt or an Instagram post—being hardcore or tough or proving the haters wrong. There are lots of superficial reasons, too, the ones you'll never share on a status update. We all have them!

WHAT SUPERFICIAL REASON DREW YOU INTO THE SPORT?

» *"#It'sbettertolookgoodthanfeelgood is my personal hashtag."* – Marjan

» *"Peer Pressure."* – Susie

» *"Bragging Rights."* – Sheryl

Finally, you have the "deep down" why, the reason you don't want to share.

Whatever your reason, it needs to be big and powerful. It has to keep you from shutting off the alarm or (frequently) skipping sessions for happy hour.

Takeaway: Tap into your reasons for tri-ing. Often there will be an external, superficial why (look hot for summer!) and then an internal more private why (to prove that I'm not a quitter!). List them, even if you don't want to share them publicly.

WHY DID YOU GET STARTED IN TRIATHLON?

» *I did my first tri because of peer pressure; all my friends were racing, so I figured I'd give it a shot. I broke my ankle and both leg bones in my first race (bike wreck—and I had been worried about the ocean swim). After that, it was a personal challenge to come back and complete a tri. It took me a year to run a 5K again, and then I did my tri "just to finish what I started" and was hooked! – Becky*

MY CHANGING WHY

After John and I got hooked on the sport in 2009, it wasn't all roses and champagne. As with any journey, there were ups and downs, twists and turns. My why changed over time along with life.

At first, I craved accomplishment and excitement. I inherently enjoyed competing with myself, striving to reach goals that seemed impossible. Triathlon was a stream of endless dopamine hits with every session checked off and every PR reached. Endurance sports helped me achieve a flow state and took the edge off my Type A personality.

My second Kona qualification at IRONMAN Louisville 2013

From an extrinsic perspective, I enjoyed competing against others. But over the next few years, external rewards began to play a greater role and eroded my inherent enjoyment of the sport. I was like the rat pushing the lever in the Skinner Box— sometimes the push would lead to a reward (a good race), but other times I was left unsatisfied.

Eventually, even if I performed well, it felt hollow and unsatisfying. Instead of being happy with success, I focused only on areas where I was lacking. I never—not even one time— finished a race and thought, "I am proud of how I did." Even if I won, I would secretly think "it was only because so-and-so didn't show up" or "everyone else was tired from training."

Over time, I invested in coaching others rather than focusing on my own personal performances only. This happened gradually and organically. Seeing others succeed *was* a satisfying, sustainable reward. And seeing lives change in ways beyond a finish line was a greater reward still.

My original why—the pursuit of an impossible challenge—wasn't gone. I sought that experience in other areas of life. In a roundabout way, that's how I came to write this book.

Takeaway: Think about your sources of intrinsic and extrinsic motivation and pick a few to apply to the following list.

» List all your sources of motivation.

» Now pare down to the BIGGEST reasons (2-4).

» For each, identify as extrinsic or intrinsic.

» Is this source likely to be motivational over a long period of time?

» Is this source of motivation healthy?

Training can be a healthy outlet when the inevitable stressors of life rear their ugly heads. That's exactly what Deirdre, my wonderful friend and athlete, has found throughout her journey.

#TriCourage Story: Deirdre's Triathlon Journey

—By Deirdre DeKock

Deirdre rocking IRONMAN Arizona

When I started triathlon eight years ago, I was a young mother and had just lost my father. I hit a low point and felt I had no identity. I tried running, but I wasn't getting fulfillment until my now ex-husband introduced me to triathlon.

Triathlon has challenged and pushed me harder than anything else in my life. I have to dig deep physically and mentally on a daily basis since there are a thousand reasons to skip an early morning swim or that last mile of a long run.

In the beginning, I had every excuse not to tri: young children at home, a husband who was traveling Monday through Friday, and all the bumps, bruises, and broken bones that come with the sport (falling off your bike is a fantastic way to break your arm). I had every excuse to quit, but I didn't. Every obstacle I overcame brought me closer to realizing triathlon was something I had control over. My results were mine and mine alone. What I put into the sport was exactly what I got out of it. In time, I learned whatever I put into *all* aspects of my life was exactly what I got out of it.

While learning this lesson, I entered a difficult time. Our family moved to another city, and my marriage of seventeen years came to an end. I didn't have my old support group by my side. They couldn't hold me accountable on those hard mornings when I'd rather just crawl in bed, cry, and give up (and, yes, those days did and do still happen). Again I had the choice to make excuses or to use the lessons I learned.

I am much STRONGER than I think, and I can face this new challenge. In time, I discovered a triathlon support group in my new town. Still, in the back of my head, I was planning my exit from triathlons, because life was just too hard.

One day my coach and my best friend convinced me to do a last-minute IRONMAN 70.3. I decided this would be the perfect exit from triathlon. I went into the race with no expectations other than that it would be another "therapy session" and that I would enjoy every moment of it.

During the run portion, I ran with a guy named Sergio Y. He played cat and mouse with me that day. I told him we had to dig deep and finish this race together. He said he was in too much pain and that he could not do it, but I told him to take it "mile by mile."

It was then I realized the only way we will ever reach goals in life is to take it day by day. That race, I qualified for the 70.3 World Championships. Apparently, God wasn't ready for me to give up triathlon or on myself. He knew I needed something on which to focus and to teach me important life lessons.

Triathlon has taught me so much, and it helps me find myself when I feel lost. God has shown me just how STRONG I am, and He has taught me to get to the finish line one mile at a time. God has a wonderful plan for me, and if I can help one person find something they love through my journey, I know I will glorify Him.

3

HOW TRI CAN CHANGE YOU

> *"No discipline seems pleasant at the time, but painful. Later on, however, it produces a harvest of righteousness and peace for those who have been trained by it."* –Hebrews 12:11

Training and completing an event can impact your life in unusual ways. That's what happened to Debbie, once a talented college swimmer. In her twenties, she worked a job she hated with 25 extra pounds on her frame. As she put it, she was "very out of shape." Debbie knew something had to change.

"I was feeling incredibly depressed, overweight, and in a huge funk," said Debbie. Needing something big to propel her out of a rut, Debbie decided to register for a half-iron distance race she'd found.

"I was shaking as I was registering for it and feeling like I had lost my mind (I'm sure there was a glass or two of wine in there for courage). Once I pressed submit and got my confirmation email, it was real. From that day forward, I started exercising again."

Knowing little about training, Debbie "fumbled" through her first tri but finished. After that she was hooked. She joined a tri club, dropped over an hour off her 70.3 time, and even signed up for an IRONMAN. Yet Debbie says the biggest changes in her life went beyond race times or becoming physically fit. "Triathlon training helped me get healthy, but also provided structure and confidence. I was able to get a new job, coordinate my schedule to accommodate training, and become empowered. I learned I don't have to settle for anything."

TERMS TO KNOW

Half Iron Distance, IRONMAN 70.3, or 70.3—These terms denote a 1.2-mile swim, a 56-mile bike, and a 13.1-mile run. Since the term 70.3 is trademarked by the World Triathlon Corporation (IRONMAN), independent races of this distance are called half-iron distance instead.

Iron Distance versus IRONMAN versus 140.6—These terms indicate a 2.4-mile swim, a 112-mile bike, and a 26.2-mile run. The terms IRONMAN and 140.6 are both trademarked by the World Triathlon Corporation, so independent races of this distance are called iron distance.

SMALL CHANGE CAN LEAD TO BIG CHANGE

Often, a small change (like racing a 5K) leads to greater change along the way (like changing jobs or outlook on life). My friend Kathryn and I became enamored with this idea and used this principle as the premise of our podcast, *Grit and Dirt* (gritanddirt. com). There we share stories of people who have changed their lives (grit) and the steps you can take to do it for yourself (dirt).

Many elements of the stories are similar. They start with someone who felt stuck in an area of life: a dead-end job, a dysfunctional relationship, an addiction, or lack of excitement and purpose. Then, an interruption or habit change disrupts their routine, leading to a huge shift in the way they live their lives.

This phenomenon can be applied to habits in all areas of life. It makes sense. If you're trying to change a pattern, replacing it with a new behavior is more effective than simply *not* doing the problem behavior.

DANI'S LIFE CHANGES

Told by her doctor to lose 70 pounds, Dani braved the gym, reluctantly at first. There she met a friendly and helpful group of triathletes who invited her to ride 40 miles at nearby Stone Mountain, which is as hilly as the name suggests. Dani had been on exactly one flat bike ride before, but showed up anyway.

Dani struggled—hard—yet the ride changed the course of her life. It was difficult, but she did it anyway. It boosted her confidence for her next challenge, and gradually her self-talk began to change. "Instead of saying I *might* do something, I replaced it with I *will* run a half marathon, or I *am* going to become the first woman to do X."

Dani eventually discovered cycling was a talent, a passion that led to amazing athletic feats. She was part of a two-female record-setting team at the Ride Across America and set a time trial record riding across the state of Florida. More recently she became the first female to complete Epic 5— a race that features five iron distance triathlons in five days across the five islands of Hawaii.

"Once I did something, and it wasn't that bad, I was like, I wonder what else I can do? I got really curious about what I was capable of doing." – Dani Grabol

Beyond record-setting rides, triathlon taught Dani life lessons. "Endurance sports teach you discipline, and it bleeds over into every aspect of life. You look at leaders—successful people—they are generally disciplined and don't give up on things easily."

#TriLessons: How Tri-ing Changed Me

When I started triathlon, I worked a job I didn't love that required skills and behavior the opposite of my natural personality. Still, it was a good job—benefits, a company car, a quarterly bonus. How could I complain? I was fortunate, blessed to have the opportunities I'd been given. But the more I continued down my chosen path, sales, the less appealing the destination looked.

Part of what held me back was guilt. Shouldn't I have it figured out already? Instead, I had a hodgepodge of experiences that made me an expert in nothing.

I endured a short stint in law school, where I was reminded I'm a talented test taker but terrible at details (read: I smoked the LSAT (Law School Admissions Test) but sucked at everything that came after). I taught LSAT prep, which was as fun as it sounds.

After that, I tackled graduate classes in counseling where I remembered I enjoy being a listening ear to friends but not to total strangers. I also nabbed a master's in health promotion, but it never turned into an actual job. I fell back on personal training, which I enjoyed as a stopgap but couldn't imagine doing forever.

Ultimately, my love of triathlon and endurance sports shaped my path and continues to do so. Triathlon wasn't *the answer,* but it was the thing that got me to the thing. It helped me realize I already have the tools to live out my purpose, wherever life takes me. Here are a few life lessons triathlon has taught me.

Lesson 1: Keep Going When It Hurts.

Be joyful in hope, patient in affliction, faithful in prayer.
–Romans 12:12

At IRONMAN St George 2012, race morning started with ideal conditions. The pros began their swim in calm waters. Next, the horn sounded for the age groupers. Five minutes later, a powerful windstorm hit. The strangest thing about it was the timing. If it started any earlier, the swim would have been delayed or canceled. But instead, it blew in just as the age groupers reached the point of no return.

John, who was spectating, said you could see the clouds coming over the horizon. Just like that, our idyllic day turned into *The Perfect Storm.*

I couldn't see one other person much less figure out where to swim with any degree of accuracy. When you sighted, the droplets hitting your face hurt, like riding a jet ski in a rainstorm. We were supposed to swim around an island. Countless age groupers were told to get back in when they arrived at the shore, having no idea that they'd missed the island completely. A few volunteers were even told the race was over, so they plucked age groupers out of the water, ending their races then and there.

I made it through that swim through God's grace and my trusty wetsuit. Eventually the shore arrived, and it was time for the bike ride. The first several hours were pure headwind. Three hours and thirty minutes in, I'd only ridden 40 miles, below the average pace I needed to make the cutoff. Because I was slower than expected, it also was much longer between aid stations.

I clearly remember swerving around a dusty desert canyon road, with nothing left to drink but Red Bull, hallucinating about possible excuses I could make to stop. Quit. The only justifiable excuse I came up with was if I literally crashed off the side of the road.

In the end I didn't crash, and I made it to the finish line—sore, dehydrated, and with a permanent seam mark branded in my rear end from too long in the saddle. There was a 33% DNF (Did Not Finish) rate—the highest of any IRONMAN to date.

That day I learned a lesson in perseverance. Sure, I'd hurt many times in training and racing, but that was the farthest I'd been pushed. Sometimes life just hurts, and the only thing you can do is keep going.

Lesson 2: Process Versus Outcome.

And let us not grow weary of doing good, for in due season we will reap, if we do not give up. –Galatians 6:9

You can control your training, your preparation, and your attitude. Other things you cannot, like mechanicals, bad weather, and illness.

At IRONMAN Chattanooga 2014, I DNF'd because of a mechanical. That incident taught me to be more prepared, to improve my process. During IRONMAN Chattanooga 70.3 2015, I got a giant hole in my tire. I had no dollar bill to plug the hole. So instead I screamed by the side of the road like a crazy person until I was tossed a used gel wrapper, which I macgyvered to successfully plug the hole in my tire.

Racing turned into spectating during the IRONMAN Chattanooga 2014.

What's my point? Continually improving your process and preparation should be the goal. But there are always things out of your control to keep you from having "the perfect day."

The same things happen in daily life. You prepped for your big presentation for weeks, then your boss asks someone else to step in. You planned the perfect holiday or family gathering, and instead Uncle Jean started the same old argument and ruined it. As easy as it is to say and as hard as it is to do, the only thing you can do is control your preparation and your attitude.

Lesson 3: Facing Fears.

For God gave us not a spirit of fearfulness; but of power and love and discipline. – 2 Timothy 1:7

Committing to a goal means sharing it. For a long time, I was scared to say I was writing a book. Before that I was embarrassed to admit I wanted to qualify for Kona. And prior to *that*, I was reluctant to share I hoped to complete a triathlon. Why? Because they were huge stretch goals—so far out of reach that someone, somewhere, would smirk and think "what makes her think she can do that?"

Getting over fear involves putting yourself out there. Start in small ways. Since triathlon involves tons of tiny goals, it can help you get better at loudly proclaiming your goals from the rooftops.

Lesson 4: Developing Discipline.

Whatever your hand finds to do, do it with all your might. – Ecclesiastes 9:10

Daily drudgery is part of even the most exciting goals. Want to cross the finish line of a triathlon? It will involve some 5AM wakeups and chilly pools. Want to publish a book? That's going to involve a host of rejections and revisions along the way. Triathlon instills discipline for the big stuff and the day to day grind.

Takeaway: Training and racing will shake your status quo. Whether you're in an exercise rut or a life rut, the mere act of changing one thing can have enormous consequences. Triathlon can also teach valuable life lessons.

TERMS TO KNOW

Sighting—Navigating the course while swimming, without breaking stroke.

Age Groupers—Refers to athletes competing in five-year age categories (e.g., 40-44). Used as a catchall term for those athletes not competing as professionals.

4

OVERCOMING OBSTACLES

I blamed my triathlon "false start" on obstacles. I had too many to overcome. I didn't know how to train, bikes were expensive, and the whole thing was way too time consuming.

Right. In truth, I *could* have saved my money instead of blowing it on tacos and going out four nights a week. I'm sure someone would have let me borrow a bike. And I could have learned the information I lacked. And time? Please. I was a journalism major—chosen mostly for the absence of homework—and only worked part time. I had nothing *but* time!

Fast forward seven years, and the obstacles weren't much different. I may have had *less* money due to adult bills and less tolerance for overdrafting my bank account. I still didn't know a thing about triathlon, and I was working full time. Yet I had plenty of time to train and race; I just had to find it. The difference was the commitment level. In school my dream was just an empty idea; in adulthood I committed to my goals.

Do you have tougher obstacles to overcome? Quite possibly. The challenges of caregiving, frequent travel, and competing responsibilities compound everyday hurdles. In this chapter we'll identify a few of the most common stumbling blocks.

WRITE DOWN OBSTACLES

You're probably thinking of ten excuses already: you're too old, too busy, not athletic. As an exercise, list the top three reasons why you should NOT attempt your goal and keep them handy. No need to do anything else, just file them away. Here are few common obstacles. Recognize yourself in any?

"I'M TOO OLD."

"Age is just a number. It shouldn't discourage one from trying something new. It feels good to do something for yourself that you never thought of doing. The psychic and physical payoff is tremendous: You sleep better, eat better, worry less, and are more positive." – Sibyl Jacobson

Think you're too old to try something new? You may be surprised at the wide age range that triathlon attracts. In our triathlon club, we've had members ranging from their 20s to 70s, and that age range expands all the time. Earlier we introduced Sybil Jacobson, age 74, who won her age group at IRONMAN 70.3 Worlds in Chattanooga. The retired insurance executive cites several benefits to starting later in life such as having more available time, disposable income, and a life perspective that comes in handy when things go wrong.

Sybil at the 2017 USA Triathlon National Championships

Jacobson isn't the only one tri-ing. You may have heard of Sister Madonna Buder dubbed "Iron Nun." At age 82, Buder finished Subaru IRONMAN Canada, becoming the world record holder of the oldest woman to finish an IRONMAN triathlon. Not only that, she's still tri-ing to this day, recently grabbing headlines for finishing the Age Group National Championship run leg without shoes (she forgot them). Perhaps the most impressive thing about

Buder is that she didn't start tri-ing until age 48. Is it because 48 is so old? No way. It's because many 38- and even 28-year-olds are already using the excuse "I'm too old."

Takeaway: Age alone is *no* excuse not to give triathlon a go. Book an appointment with your physician to make sure you're healthy enough to start training, then toss that excuse.

"I'M NOT ATHLETIC."

Kat Gurd never considered herself an athlete. As a kid, she avoided sports save for a season of softball, which only reinforced her dislike. Kat says, "I was never engaged in anything, and I had weight struggles my whole life."

After college, Kat braved the gym in an attempt to lose weight but it was never "fun." Her motivation was simply controlling calories and weight.

All that changed the day Kat heard a commercial on the radio for an ovarian cancer fundraising ride. She had lost an aunt to ovarian cancer who was diagnosed at 35 and passed away 16 years later. The cause resonated with Kat, especially because she herself was the same age as when her aunt was diagnosed.

The fundraising ride was a virtual training program culminating in a six-hour indoor ride, all to raise funds for ovarian cancer. Kat trained and completed the event, but after, she wanted more, saying, "I found a side of me that I didn't know existed, and it began a process of breaking my own mental boundaries about what I thought I could do." Over a series of years, Kat completed a succession of races including 5Ks, 10Ks, and half marathons, plus three full marathons and an IRONMAN.

Takeaway: Kat found the athlete inside her along the way. Could it be that way for you, too?

"I CAN'T SWIM."

Jenna Mink recently completed IRONMAN Louisville, which included a 2.4-mile river swim, yet she started out a non-swimmer. "When I decided I wanted to tri, I was terrified of swimming. I seriously dreaded the pool and found all sorts of excuses to skip swim training." What changed her path? She found a group with which she felt comfortable then diligently practiced. Now she rarely misses a swim on her training schedule.

Takeaway: Don't let a fear or lack of swim experience deter you from starting. Thousands of grown adults learn to swim every year, and you can, too! Learn the right way by searching for a learn-to-swim class or swim lessons in your area. Be patient with yourself and commit to practicing.

"I'M TOO BROKE."

Triathlon can be expensive, but it's possible to train and race on a budget. Carolina did her first triathlon (almost) for free. She used an old bike that someone gave her, borrowed a tri suit, and walked all the hills because she couldn't shift gears. And Shana did her first triathlon with a swimsuit and shorts she bought for $10 on eBay and a Walmart mountain bike.

Takeaway: The shiny, flashy bikes stick out at a race. But if you look harder, you can see many athletes racing on a budget. You can start training today with a pair of goggles, any type of bike (borrowed or owned), and a good pair of running shoes.

"I'M TOO BUSY."

Finding time to train is tough. In Rachel's case, she has to plan especially well. "I'm a runner who does three to four marathons a year and some shorter distances. I train with a coach. I own a business, have two teenagers, and am on two national boards. Plus, I travel once or twice a month."

What's key for Rachel is prioritizing. "I use TrainingPeaks to schedule a week ahead so I can plan, and I know I'm most successful at early morning training. I lay out my clothes at night to remove early morning hurdles. My family respects all my efforts and what they produce, so that helps tremendously! I also try hard to be kind to myself when things go sideways."

Nearly everyone is too busy to fit in training. No really. It's not about "having" time; it's about making time by dropping or shuffling other things. Maybe your training can take place while you catch up on your favorite show, or maybe you'll regularly stare 4 AM in the face. If you can find 30 to 45 minutes, five days a week, then you can prepare adequately for your sprint triathlon. That's about the amount of exercise recommended for good health, too!

"I'M ROLLING SOLO."

It is easier to enter the world of tri if your partner or friends are already involved. I was fortunate to have John, my partner in crime, throughout the journey. However, it's not necessary or even common to have friends or a spouse that live, eat, and sleep tri. You may be surprised by how quickly you find new friends who support your efforts.

"I'M TOO HEAVY."

Marilia Bocchetto has a successful career as a writer, editor, and producer for *CNN*. She is also a triathlete, having finished the NYC triathlon and other events. But she didn't start out as an athlete.

In 2014 Maria found herself weighing 300 pounds. Although she went on various diets and exercised sporadically, she struggled to keep the weight off. But she knew something had to change. After making the life-changing decision to have bariatric surgery, Marilia had her turning point. Once she was approved for surgery, she began changing her habits in preparation for her new lifestyle.

After having the surgery, Marilia completed her first triathlon as well as the NYC Olympic Triathlon. Marilia's regret was not starting sooner and letting her weight stop her. "Don't make the same mistakes I made," she advises. "I let my weight dictate the things I did and didn't do."

Marilia before her first triathlon in 2016, The Tall Pines Sprint. It would be her first open water swim, first competitive bike ride, and first triathlon finish.

Start where you are, even if you're beginning from a position of low physical fitness, or far from the weight you want to be. If you remain committed, you *can* reach your goals!

"I'M TOO SCARED."

Candace Doby has done many things others would find courageous. She was a high-level track and field athlete during her senior year of college, she moved alone to a new state without a plan at age 25, and her first trip abroad was to Indonesia, alone. Now Candace's mission is to empower girls and women to embrace courage in school, work, and play.

Eight years ago, Candace became interested in the construct of courage itself. How can people summon it at will? Since the opposite of courage is fear, living with courage naturally denotes overcoming a state of fear. Candace found that "the unknown" was a huge trigger for fear. Applied to something like a race, the unknown includes questions such as, "How will my body feel during the race? Can it withstand running this distance?"

"Don't just let fear run wild, get information," recommends Candace. Getting information is the first step to building the confidence you need to address the goal. The next step is to practice by taking small risks then building off of successful attempts. You build your ability to be able to say, "I have the confidence to do it." Each time you stretch your limits, you're building the essential confidence that will then allow you to take the subsequent step.

Lindsay Waibel took small steps to reach her bigger goal. In her mid-thirties, Waibel found herself unexpectedly facing a divorce. Looking for something to improve her self-confidence, she signed up for a half marathon. She didn't have a fancy training plan or much of a plan at all. "I just thought I would put on my running shoes and see how far I could run, going farther each time." After accomplishing her goal Waibel found that the half marathon wasn't enough, and she wanted more.

Using that race as a stepping stone, Lindsay has since completed four marathons, an IRONMAN, and more. "Believe in yourself and take the time to invest just half an hour a few times a week," says Lindsay. "You don't have to start with a half marathon."

Takeaway: We all have obstacles to reaching our goals, and many of them can be overcome.

One obstacle most of us have experienced is inertia. A body at rest wants to stay at rest, and the hardest you'll ever work is taking those first steps. Once you're moving, it's easier to keep up that drive. Dusty Scott has experienced this very phenomenon.

#TriCourage: Dusty Scott on Overcoming Inertia

—By Dusty Scott

How to Kill a Wolverine

How do you kill a wolverine? Give it everything it wants. Put it in a large, comfortable enclosure with a plush den, all the rodents and caribou steaks it wants, keep the temperature perfect, and wait. It might take a year or two, but it will die. Without the need to hunt, it will not hunt. Without the need to find shelter, it won't worry about things like digging holes. Soon it will lose interest in those things, actually lose the ability to do those things, and then you'll have yourself a nice throw rug/conversation piece that started when you posited a theory that life requires a challenge to thrive. Don't kill a wolverine. They're hard to catch (and even if you do catch one, you will instantly regret it), and they really don't deserve it.

Here's the mind-blowing part: The same rule applies to people. It's pretty simple: We need resistance in order to grow muscles, minds, skills, self-worth, relationships, and so on. My story isn't particularly inspiring, but as such, it is exquisitely relatable. We are all inspired by people overcoming incredible adversity, but we should be glad and feel fortunate to be in the majority of folks who don't have a genetic defect, abusive parents, or a horrendous accident to prod us to greatness. On the other hand, we have zero excuses not to, and it is kind of a cosmic crime not to push yourself in some way just because you haven't had some unspeakable tragedy befall you.

I was in my late thirties when I started connecting the dots that I wish I had connected in my twenties. I was working as a sort of graphic artist savant weirdo for a software company, making enough money to live comfortably, living in a cool condominium, driving a decent car, and enjoying all the things I "needed." I was also getting a little soft in a lot of ways. I wasn't getting any exercise or eating particularly well, doing what it took to get by at work while staying under the radar, and even starting to avoid relationships because I didn't need anything rocking my boat. That boat had large letters emblazoned across the transom: "COMFORT ZONE."

The comfort zone is the worst place for people to be long-term, and it is pretty much what our society is built around. Cars that park themselves so we don't have to bother with annoying things like learning a skill, instant access to any product or food we want without the risk of having to leave the house and possibly socialize, and myriad other conveniences are reducing the number of things we have to do for ourselves. Don't get me wrong—these things are great and I'm glad they exist. I'm not saying we need to go back to the days when an evening activity was eating rabbit skeleton soup and watching your siblings die. This isn't suffering for suffering's sake. It's the idea of adding some healthy discomfort to your life.

Shortly after this light bulb went on, I went to my boss and quit my job to pursue a different career. That sentence makes it sound like it was easy, but I assure you it was not. I spent weeks agonizing over it, fearful of the unknown, and finally realized that I wasn't afraid of the change, but rather making the change. I had a feeling that as soon as I walked out of his office, I wouldn't feel like vomiting anymore. I really wanted to stop feeling like vomiting, and I was right—I felt like a million bucks when I left. A million, nervous, unsure excited bucks. In fact, looking back on all the changes I and everyone I know have made, nobody has regretted making the change even if their plans failed. However, there are many people with bitter regrets because they never tried. I'd rather be part of the former group.

This was the catalyst that eventually got me started toward steering my life. Once I realized I had the guts to make a big decision, I decided to get married. Now I had two changes under my belt, and like most other things, it was getting a little easier each time. A year or so later my wife Sara (who could ride a bike when we got married, but not a bike with gears to shift) started hanging around with a group of lovable crazy people I came to know as "Triathletes." I admired her tenacity, which turned to competency, then success, then a passion for a sport that I had seen on television and clearly knew was strictly for people who were not me. I had three back surgeries in my recent past due to discs fragmenting and figured it was a matter of time before I could no longer walk on my own, so why tempt fate? I was also getting fat…and all of this seemed like a lot of work.

There are a million reasons not to do a billion things, and the sad human impulse is a strange oppositional defiance. "I can't afford it," "I travel too much," "I have a rare condition," or whatever else we come up with. It is such a hardwired response in people that once you start noticing, it will drive you insane. So you're welcome. The good thing about being irritated by it is that you will notice it in your own behavior and not allow yourself to take part in it. That alone will make you a better person.

At age 41 I got a pair of shoes and a wristband that counted my steps and decided I'd do 10,000 steps a day. If I was feeling good, I'd jog for a couple of minutes. When I traveled, I would walk around a strange city for an hour or so. If that wasn't an option, I'd walk on the treadmill at the hotel. In the rare instances that I didn't have time for either, I'd stretch or do push-ups or try to follow along with a yoga video on YouTube.

My very simple goal was to get sweaty every day I possibly could. I soon grew extremely annoyed when I heard people say "I don't have time" for things. By "time," they invariably meant "the desire"…which is acceptable, but please be honest for god's sake. There is not a single person who doesn't waste 20 minutes a day doing something meaningless, so that is one excuse I can't handle coming from an adult's mouth. If someone says, "I don't want to," then fine…but I'm still going to bug you about it.

One day Sara asked me if I wanted to go swimming with her. I got the word "no" about halfway out before I resorbed it because I had trained myself to abhor excuses. In the past few months, I had gone from barely being able to walk a mile to running a mile with no problem aside from not enjoying it at all. Let's see if swimming sucks as much as everyone says. I mean, it's a very uncomfortable thought, so by definition, it will be good for me. I was right all the way around. It was exhausting and weird and felt unnatural, and I got water in every orifice, and I really, really sucked at it, but at least I looked ridiculous doing it, right? I sort of amazed myself when I had the thought leaving the pool, "I might be the worst swimmer on earth. I can't wait to go back and try again."

My outlook had been evolving for a couple of years now, but that was the first time I realized that I had fostered an instinct to pursue discomfort—one of the greatest feelings I've ever had.

I wish I could tell you that I was now running a seven-minute mile and had some podium spots at various triathlons and they were considering naming a shoe after me, but none of that is true (hey, I said this was relatable, didn't I?). What I did by age 43 was turn myself into a healthy person who was a slow runner, average swimmer, and below-average cyclist. I did a half Ironman and finished before everyone went home, and I am now one of those crazy people I used to only watch on TV. The most important thing that I accomplished by far was to abolish a lifelong fear of discomfort and change. It is so ingrained in me now that I actually start each day with a cold shower. By the time I have breakfast, I have already done something I didn't want to do, and as insane as that sounds, it has a very definite purpose. (And if you think coffee wakes you up, try a cold shower. You have no idea.) My coworkers know that I run or swim almost every day when we travel, so the assumption is that I love it. "You must love running to go do it every day…" I can say honestly that my feelings about running range from "I wish I was doing something else" to "I would literally rather be on fire right now." What I love is hating it and doing it anyway. The satisfaction that comes from that is immense.

This is supposed to be about exercise, and I guess it is. It is also about the book you want to write or the business you want to start. You can't start any earlier than right now, so start looking for the things that make you the most uncomfortable and work on those. Once you're comfortable with the idea of discomfort, you'll be amazed what you can do.

Now let's take a look at another type of barrier, a physical one. We've all dealt with, if not injury, our body not working as perfectly as we'd like. Jenny was a talented athlete devastated by her condition who went on to find meaning through endurance sports.

#TriCourage: Jenny Overcame Injury

—By Jenny Johnson

My journey with osteochondritis dissecans (OCD)—a joint condition where bone underneath cartilage dies due to lack of blood flow—started at the young age of 13. At 13, there was a possibility that the condition would heal itself since I was so young. With high hopes, the doctor handed me a pair of crutches and said to come back in six months.

Yep, you heard it right, six months on crutches with "hopes" of the bone healing itself; there went my freshman year of basketball. I remember returning to the doctor later that spring, and, of course, I told the doctor that I felt great! Little did he know that I had unbearable pain in my right knee, but I wasn't going to tell him that for fear of being put back on crutches and losing yet another season of basketball. After all, I had a college scholarship to train for.

Fast forward four years, and there I was, senior year of high school, All-State basketball team, headed to the All-Star game, and a college basketball offer in my hands. I had made it! Or had I? I remember driving to our state's capital for the All-Star game, ready to prove that I was ready for the next level of competition. My knee had other plans, though. I remember making it to halftime, but I was in so much pain I just wanted to cry and quit.

I couldn't juke left or right. I couldn't stop the drive. I couldn't keep up. I was in serious pain. I remember the long drive home. I remember the disappointment in my mom's face because I didn't play hard and was lazy on defense. I remember finally breaking down. For four years, I had hidden the knee pain, I had hidden the pain medications, I had hidden the late-night Epsom salt baths and ice packs, but there was no hiding it anymore. I remember calling my college coach, explaining the situation, and officially declining my contract to play collegiate basketball. My dreams shattered, just like the bones in my knee.

Fast forward one year from my All-Star game catastrophe. There I am, sitting in a waiting room in Birmingham, Alabama, waiting to see yet another specialist to diagnose me and give me my "options" for treatment. I remember Dr. James Andrews and Dr. Lyle Cain reading my X-rays and MRIs, in complete shock at the 2-inch hole in my femur. "You'll never run again." I remember it like it was yesterday. Those four simple words spoken by my orthopedic surgeon. This disease had destroyed my dreams of ever playing collegiate basketball and now even threatened my ability to ever walk normally again.

I remember hearing my options. Bone grafts were a long shot because of the severity of my OCD legion. Stem cell treatment was still in its infancy stages. I remember looking out the window with the doctor's voice just droning on in the background. After much deliberation, I was put on the transplant list. A bone transplant was risky, but it was my "best" option. Two weeks later, I got the call. They had found a donor. The surgery was hard; recovery was hell. Bed ridden for two months, crutches for nine, PT for over two years—five total surgeries in all. I was an athlete, through and through—volleyball, basketball, soccer, softball, racquetball—I thrived on the rush of competition.

But now, my greatest competition was convincing my spirit that I should eat and get out of bad each day. Depression hit hard; addiction hit harder. From 130 pounds to 105 in just nine months, I was sick, not just physically, but mentally and emotionally and spiritually. The worst part: The surgery didn't take the pain away. In fact, it made it ten times worse.

I remember going nights without sleep because of the pain. I remember throwing up time and time again because of the heavy doses of oxycontin, hydrocodone, and morphine being pumped through my system. As each day passed, the healing slowly began. I busted it in PT. I was diligent. I never missed an exercise. I was going to run again—they just didn't realize it yet.

As the physical healing began, so did the emotional. The depression broke; the addiction to pain meds was overcome. The next step to healing was buying my first bicycle. Recommended by Dr. Cain, cycling would be a phenomenal way for me to exercise since it is a low-impact sport. I remember my first group ride—four total falls in clip-in shoes.

My legs were so weak from the muscle atrophy that I couldn't keep up. Three total group rides, and I was dropped in all of them. I hated this sport! This sport was humiliating and did nothing but remind me of how much fitness I had lost. So, I hung it up, and for three years my bike hung on my wall, collecting dust.

I graduated college from Clemson University (Go Tigers!) and moved to Atlanta. Call it perfect timing or divine intervention, but every corner I turned, I met cyclists. I started doing group rides. By now I was a bit stronger because it had been five years since my last surgery. I was slowly catching the bike "fever."

And then, my first sprint triathlon. I was hooked! I was the last out of the water (did I mention I didn't learn how to swim until I was 24 years old because of my tremendous fear of water?), I was slow on the bike, and I was even slower on the run. But I didn't care. I was running again! I was competing again! I was nearly dead last, but I was grinning from ear to ear. The rest is history.

Three months later I registered for my first Ironman race—Ironman Louisville. From sprint to full distance, I was going big or going home. I was going to prove to the doctors that I would run again! I was going to prove to myself that I was an overcomer. So, I trained. I trained hard. 4AM masters swim classes. Two-a-day workouts for strength training and rehabilitation. Long weekends spent in the saddle. And, most importantly, strategic run workouts and constant communication with my coach (Meghan Fillnow with Fillnow Coaching) to make sure we were building a strong base and increasing my mileage at just the right times. In July 2014, I had my first podium—3rd Overall Female at the Chattahoochee Challenge Olympic Triathlon. By August 24, 2014, I was ready to conquer my first 140.6. I swam 2.4 miles. I biked 112 miles. And yes, I RAN 26.2 miles! I crossed that finish line. And I'll never forget those four simple words, "You are an Ironman."

Jenny celebrates a podium finish after the Chattahoochee Challenge triathlon.

Unfortunately, however, my journey with OCD will be lifelong. In 2015, the doctors found once again that my transplant was failing as I was beginning to have more pain and more debris locking my joints. In December 2015, I once again was given "options." Stem cell research had developed, but it was still a bit too early to go this route. Now 26 years old, I was still much too young for a knee replacement. My best option—subchondroplasty.

Like a sink hole in the road, my knee was collapsing from the inside out. The doctor's best course of action was to go in under the cartilage in efforts of reinforcing the bone inside my femur. This wouldn't fix my issues, but it would potentially buy me some much needed time until stem cell treatment was developed enough to become a viable course of action. So, here I am, a year outside of subchondroplasty surgery, PT is officially over, and I have my eyes set on conquering Augusta 70.3. This time, my training will be full of cycling, swimming, and crosstraining. My running miles will be limited. I know I won't be seeing a podium finish anytime soon, but I am okay with that. I am competing again, and for that, I am grateful.

From "You'll never run again" to "You are an Ironman," I had defied the odds. I had proven the doctors wrong. I had achieved my goal—not by my strength, but through the strength and healing of the Lord Himself. I truly believe that the Lord gives and takes away. He took away my dreams of college basketball, but He gave me a passion for triathlon that I would have never found otherwise.

The friends I have met through this sport have been a blessing. The lessons I have learned have been irreplaceable. I am thankful for my disease—for what it has taught me, for the strength it has given me, for the relationships it has brought me, for the love of triathlon it has instilled within me. Every time I step up to the start line, I am overwhelmed with the ability to compete. Every time I cross the finish line, I am reminded that hard work pays off and that miracles of healing do happen. Never give up! Never say never!

5

MOMS WHO TRI

When Kat Gurd had her daughter, she had been a triathlete for many years. "There were times when I was more committed to it than others," explains Kat, "but when I had Hailey, I decided to get back in shape with triathlon."

Rather than completely change their lifestyle, Kat and her husband Peter incorporated Hailey, then later their son Henry, from the beginning. "We integrated her into our lives as much as possible. Hailey was spectating a race when she was three weeks old!"

How can other moms get back to training after giving birth? Since recovery timelines vary, Kat recommends talking to your doctor first. Kat began swimming at three weeks postpartum, riding the trainer at four, and running at five. And she walked around the neighborhood the day they got home from the hospital.

Once you get the green light, time management is a major challenge. Kat and Peter's strategy was splitting up training times.

Kat trains in the morning while Peter exercises in the evenings. "I got up really early," recalls Kat. "I was never into morning workouts before, but with a new baby, if I got up at five, I could train and get back home before she woke up. I wasn't missing anything that way. So even when I was on maternity leave, I found morning training I was able to do."

Kat warns things won't always go how you envision, but keeping a family calendar can help. "We set our schedules on a weekly basis and figure out how to make the week work around stuff we really want to do. Many times, between day jobs and trying to train, we may meet up at a parking lot to hand off. But it's important enough that we make it work."

For convenience and efficiency, Kat often trains in the house or as close as possible. She adds that some days, getting a workout in *at all* is a victory and should be treated as such, even if it's not perfectly aligned with a schedule.

Kat and Peter believe that though training with young children can be complicated, it's worth it. "Having this crazy schedule makes me better at all parts of my life. I give my best to everything when I am there. When I'm at work, I don't want to work longer, I want to be more efficient so I can get home to the family.

"I hear other mothers say taking time away makes them feel guilty, but I feel like having that break makes me a happier person. I feel better mentally, and when I get to see friends, it's a multipurpose social and physical outlet. I haven't felt that guilt even when I was doing long IRONMAN training. I believe it benefits my family for me to have that time away, too."

SIX TIPS FOR TRAINING WITH CHILDREN

There were two ever-present themes with nearly every mom I interviewed. The first was the myth of doing it all versus the reality of doing the best you can. Training and life often don't go exactly as planned, and perfection should not be the standard you try to meet.

The second theme was the importance of planning—planning ahead, planning contingencies, and planning backups on backups. What works best for each mother's situation is different. We enlisted tips from moms in several scenarios— moms who stay at home, moms who work outside the home, and moms who have a combo approach. Here are their top six tips:

1. GET TRAINING DONE EARLY.

Over and over we heard advice that early mornings are almost universally the preferred time to train. After that there's a much bigger chance that something will interrupt plans. Laura fit in training for IRONMANs and marathons with a full-time job and children by running a .3-mile loop around her neighborhood at 4 AM.

2. FIND WAYS TO BRING THEM ALONG.

Before Claire purchased a jogging stroller, finding times for consistent workouts was extremely difficult. Now the registered nurse and mother of two doesn't have to rely on a sitter, which was a game changer.

3. HAVE FOOD READY.

Smitha paved the way for training by ensuring there was enough food around the house at all times. "I cook batches and freeze, get extra takeaways, etc., and buy fruits like they're going out of style."

4. GET PARTNER SUPPORT.

If you have a spouse or partner, Smitha adds, "don't feel guilty about leaving the kids with them." She reminds us that the term is equal parenting, not babysitting.

5. FIND KID-FRIENDLY FACILITIES.

Marjan picked her gym based on the quality of childcare. Jaime found and uses a track where her kids run or play while she does her workout. And Smitha has her children join her (on bikes) for the last miles of her long run.

6. STICK TO A SCHEDULE.

Anne, a working single mother of one, credits setting a schedule early on as a game changer. "There is nothing better than a good night's sleep and some predictability around bed, wake, and nap times."

Takeaway: It is possible to start or continue training with children in tow. Everyone's situation is different, and there is no-one-size-fits-all solution. Having an outlet just for you can be physically and mentally rewarding. Communication and flexibility are the two ingredients that stood out during interviews with moms who make it work. Letting go of perfection or an ideal is also key.

Next, Jesica D'Avanza, new mom, runner, and marathon coach (MC) via the North American Academy of Sport Fitness Professionals (NAASFP) shares her best tips for running during pregnancy and after.

#TriLessons: rUnladylike's Tips for Pregnancy and Postpartum Running

–By Jesica D'Avanza

Jesica D'Avanza, better known as rUnladylike, is a fitness blogger and certified marathon coach who recently had her first child. After giving birth to her daughter, Jesica announced to her medical team "that was officially harder than running a marathon." As both an avid runner and coach, motherhood has given Jesica a new perspective on what it means to be a mother-runner. She shares with us more about training during and after pregnancy.

"My expectations about running during and after pregnancy were drastically different than the reality," shares Jesica. She recalls a training partner who ran all nine months, maintaining paces and a regimen close to her pre-pregnancy routine. "She was running like everyone else even though she was seven months pregnant, and she ran until the very end." Conversely, Jesica says she knew right away that her journey would be different.

Five weeks into pregnancy, Jesica's breathing was labored, and she needed walk breaks. "For me, running was a struggle from the very beginning. Instead of making me feel strong like it always does, it made me feel weak. It was a very humbling experience." Jesica struggled with comparing her paces during early pregnancy with easy and recovery runs from before. "Even running one to two minutes per mile slower than my typical easy paces was a challenge. But staying active was very important to me, so I focused on activities that felt comfortable and fulfilling, like walking, barre classes, the elliptical machine, and stationary bike."

The surprises didn't end after Jesica had her daughter. "I thought the road back would be faster," she shares. "In reality, both my mind and body needed more time. I took a very slow and conservative approach to running, which reflected my new priorities in life. This time in your life is so precious. Running can be in the background and will be there when you are ready." She implores other athletes to resist the urge to rush back into heavy training. Instead of setting big goals and deadlines immediately after pregnancy, or worse, before birth, Jesica believes that women should wait to see how they feel mentally and physically and take it slow.

Jesica gradually returned to a normal training schedule and her athletic performance has come back as well. At the time of writing this, she had completed two postpartum half marathons, surprising herself with a times that were both faster than planned. As far as specific tips for returning to training, Jesica has several:

1. When the time is right, get your baby on a structured schedule so that you both can thrive. When your child is taking good naps and sleeping through the night, it allows you to get the sleep you need to exercise early and to prevent unnecessary fatigue. Jesica credits the book *Moms on Call* for helping her develop an effective routine. "Set yourself up so that you can reclaim time for activities like running. By staying dedicated to establishing the routine, even if it's not convenient for you at first, it will make a huge impact on your entire family in the long run."

2. Complete training in the morning to maximize family time. Jesica makes sure she and her husband are present for their daughters' wakeup time at 7:30AM each day. She schedules her workouts while their daughter is sleeping, typically early in the morning before 5 or 6AM.

3. Take advantage of nap time. While your baby is sleeping, catch up on your own rest and training. They sleep a lot in the beginning!

4. Curtail expectations, especially for those first eight weeks. The first few months are wonderful and overwhelming. You'll be tired and may wonder if you'll ever feel like yourself again. You will! Your body will heal, and things will feel manageable before you know it.

5. If your budget allows, consider outsourcing time-consuming tasks such as grocery delivery, housekeeping, or meal preparation.

6. Seek support for postpartum training and racing from a credible source, such as an experienced coach or local training

group leader. It's important to start by strengthening your body to prevent muscle imbalances before building back to running. Run–walk intervals can be helpful for the first few weeks.

"Remember that you are stronger than you think and capable of more than you believe you can do. If running and racing postpartum is something you want to do, you absolutely can. Be patient with your body, take it slow and you will find your stride as your heart, body and mind are ready." – Jesica

Takeaway: Every mother's journey is different. Talk to your doctor about exercise guidelines before, during, and after pregnancy. Though it's easier said than done, be kind to yourself and avoid placing stringent expectations about what you think you "should" do.

6

FINDING ACCOUNTABILITY AND COMMUNITY

"For me, a community keeps me out of my head. Sometimes I fall victim to the voices in my head that say, "I can't" or "I don't have time." It's this community that reminds me that I can, I'm supported, and when I put in the time to train, I feel good about myself and amazed at the all the wonderful people that are part of my life. Communities let you know you're not alone, and together we accomplish so much." – Jennie

When John and I joined the tri club, we gained instant accountability. It was as simple as forking over membership dues and telling our new friends we'd be at swim practice on Monday. It took us a little bit longer to get entrenched in the community. At first it felt like a wrestling match between old friends who congregated late on weekend nights and new friends who preferred bike rides on weekend mornings. But as time passed, those two worlds came together.

Atlanta Tri Club cheer crew at the IRONMAN 70.3 World Championships
2017 in Chattanooga
© *Luis Fabian Prato*

Finding *accountability* will help you succeed in the sport and reach your goals. Finding *community* will make the whole endeavor sustainable and worthwhile. Next, we discuss the nuts and bolts of finding each.

HOW DID ACCOUNTABILITY AND COMMUNITY CHANGE YOUR TRAINING?

» *"Having a community to train with is huge. When I have a specific activity at a certain time, I have no problem getting up early, getting there, and working hard. When I don't, I start to procrastinate, and time gets lost. I was ready to quit*

> *triathlon when I found my tri club, and now, after four years, I love it as much as ever."* – Harold

» *"I signed up for my first tri by lottery with running friends. Training for my first and multiple marathons with Nike+ Run Club NYC got me motivated. It helped me stick to a plan and have lots of fun with friends along the way."* – Carolina

ACCOUNTABILITY

Success can hinge on accountability alone. And it starts by talking about your plan. Sharing is scary but also powerful. Start today by telling a friend, a coworker, or your spouse. In this section we'll discuss the specific steps to finding accountability.

HOW DID ACCOUNTABILITY HELP YOU ACHIEVE YOUR GOALS?

» *"Getting a coach was the best decision ever. I knew what to do, and she knew if I did it or not. I've had coaches for triathlon, strength training, and nutrition."* –Kathryn

» *"It helps when you promise to meet a friend at 6AM for a morning run at sub-20 degrees wind chill."* – Christopher

» *"I did a thing with two other friends: be in the gym four times a week at 6AM or you had to put $10 in the pot every day you missed."* – R.J.

ACCOUNTABILITY AND COMMUNITY: FIND IT!

Find a community where you can give and receive support. This group can be virtual or in person. Here are some starting ideas for finding accountability:

FIND (OR MAKE) A LOCAL GROUP

"I went from being a couch potato and occasional runner to a determined athlete with a purpose. Being part of a team that supports me in my goals and helps me get up when I fall is priceless. My life has a whole new meaning. I feel like I was in hibernation, and I woke up. A fish that was thrown back into the ocean!" – Elsa

On race day, triathlon is a solo effort, but training doesn't have to be. A tri club or local coaching group offers friendship and support. To start your search, check out a list of clubs registered with USA Triathlon (membership.usatriathlon.org/Public/Public/FindAClub).

There are no standard setups for tri clubs. Many exist online while others have group workouts every day of the week. Most have a variety of experience levels, whereas others may be geared toward beginner or advanced athletes. Many groups organize sponsor discounts for their members and even race-entry discounts. Some groups also offer extras like transition clinics, open water swims, and tire change clinics.

It can be intimidating to join a group the first time, but you can empower yourself by asking questions ahead of time. Here are some questions to ask:

» What is the experience level of the typical athlete?

» Are sessions organized or do you come with your own workout?

» Are sessions coach led?

» Are there group target races?

» Is there an online group or forum?

» Is the group social?

The more you know, the more confident you'll feel when you show up for your first workout. Don't be shy. Trust me. Whoever is answering your email or returning your phone call has heard your question before.

Ask about the experience levels of the group's athletes. For example, our tri club members run the gamut from very new to very experienced. And the amazing thing is, we're not the only great group in our area. Once you start searching, you may be surprised at your options.

But what if you don't have a local group? That was Allie Bachelder's situation when she first contacted me for coaching in 2014. Allie had a goal to complete a half iron distance race, and there were very few aspiring triathletes in her small town of

Decorah, Iowa. She describes that early time as challenging—frequent solo runs in zero-degree weather and long months on the bike trainer.

Allie also had *no* triathlon experience, so reaching out for online support was crucial. But when she started training, she began meeting others with similar goals at the pool and at the bike shop, ultimately founding her own group.

"I felt like after I started racing and enjoying it, I would find more and more people who were interested. It just kept growing." Today, Allie has a small local group of around 10 athletes who support each other. Some specific strategies she used included talking to athletes after races, checking out race results, and asking at her local bike shop. She even made training partners from scratch by convincing friends to tri with her.

CREATE YOUR OWN TEAM

If you opt to create your own team, here are a few things to consider:

Communication forum—Whether your group meets in person or not, you'll need a place where members can communicate freely. Sometimes the simplest solution is the best. A closed or private Facebook group is an easy, free way to get everyone excited and communicating on a regular basis. As the leader or group administrator, your job will be to get everyone engaged with training and enthusiastic about your chosen event.

Regular check-ins—Posting frequent meetups, asking questions about how other's training is going, and commiserating over any hurdles or setbacks will set the tone for everyone to share openly.

Setting a deadline—If you choose to use a Facebook group, you can create your own group-specific events to start to flesh out details and amp up the enthusiasm. For example, if your culminating event is a 5K, set up a Facebook event so that others can RSVP, talk about pre and post plans, and discuss logistics.

Regular training—Use your group to schedule in-person or virtual training events.

Takeaway: If you're not sure where to start, look up bike shops, tri shops, or run stores. A call or a visit will give you insight on the scene. Many of these stores have free workouts throughout the week. Look up tri clubs in your area on the USA Triathlon website, where you can search by club name, city, state, or discipline. IRONMAN.com (email triclub@ironman.com) also maintains a list of clubs registered with their tri club program.

TERMS TO KNOW

Strava is a popular social media network for athletes. You can share workout details with friends and give them "kudos" for their own completed sessions, as well as join teams and complete online challenges.

FIND AN ONLINE TEAM

"Strava...everyone sees every workout (or lack of a workout). If it's a good workout, I'm definitely more excited to share it. If I miss a workout, I visually see the gaps in my training week, and I don't like seeing gaps in the training schedule." – Marie

If an in-person group isn't practical, then an online one provides many of the same benefits. Beginner triathletes congregate on platforms from Meetup to Strava to Facebook. Search Facebook for groups such as Women for Tri (sponsored by IRONMAN). A quick internet search should yield dozens of options that might fit your needs.

Also check out USA Triathlon which is divided into regions and states. Each region has a women's coordinator plugged in with local, free events for women, groups, and other initiatives designed for women just like you.

RECRUIT A FRIEND

Persuading a friend to join you is a great way to make your new lifestyle fun, which then helps it stick. If you are the first of your friend group to pursue an active lifestyle, then you may initially encounter some resistance. Don't give up! They may join later after seeing the positive benefits exercise has on your life. Getting someone to sign up for an event is a huge motivator. After that they won't want to back out!

ASK FOR SUPPORT

Create your own accountability by asking friends and family for support. Abby Keenan, certified mental performance consultant with Intrepid Performance, recommends asking people in your life to fill three specific roles: cheerleader, scorekeeper, and critic. Here's how she defines each role"

»   **Cheerleader**—someone who will ONLY encourage you and offer positive feedback (related to effort, skill development, learning from mistakes, or success.)

»   **Scorekeeper**—someone who will ONLY keep track of your progress and offer factual input or ask questions related to your progress.

»   **Critic**—someone who will ONLY challenge you to push yourself more (not at the risk of injury) and offer suggestions to do so.

The role of cheerleader is a great place for family members who aren't interested in triathlon themselves. The roles of scorekeeper and critic can often be best filled in by a mentor or coach.

Takeaway: Support can come in many forms. If you're friendly and persistent, you can make a community happen whether it's primarily online or in-person.

Kathryn, my *Grit and Dirt* podcast partner and fellow triathlon coach, is entrenched in the local tri community. But once she was new in town, searching for a group of her own.

#TriCourage Story:
How Kathryn Found Community

—By Kathryn Taylor

Kathryn's confidence increased after surviving her first few group rides.

I remember the day I decided that triathlon was going to go from a "someday" idea (i.e., will never really happen) to an actual "this is the year" goal. I was 35 years old in a new city with no job, barely a single friend to call and living in my parents' house. I had been through a terrible two-year season of transition, and I wondered if I would ever have a life that felt like my own again. I had to do something different.

For some reason, that something different was a triathlon. I looked up "Triathlon Atlanta" and Team in Training came up. I had never heard of Team in Training, but it checked the boxes: be coached to do a triathlon in a cool place with a group of people while raising money for a worthy cause. So, a few days later, I showed up at the very first info meeting having no idea what to expect.

As an introvert by nature, walking into a group of people knowing no one is not my favorite thing to do. Even though I had swum as a kid and done some casual biking and running, I was sure I was going to be walking into a room of super-fit people who would make me want to curl up in the corner and eat cheese fries to hide my inadequacies. I thought of about 12 different excuses to skip the info meeting, but all of them would result in yet another marathon of reality tv shows with my parents, so I sucked it up and went.

By the end of the night I was excited to join the team. I had a few great conversations with some people who looked fit but were really nervous about swimming (whew, I had one advantage at least). I had heard stories of inspiration about why people supported the cause and most of all, I had met competent coaches.

The first session went well. It was a swim, and even though I wasn't excited to be wearing a bathing suit in front of a group of strangers, I felt like I could at least make it up and down the pool. That night was a confidence builder because I was actually moved up a few lanes.

The second workout didn't go quite as well. I got lost on my way and was late. I HATE being late. I also learned that "wheels down" in a triathlon group means, we leave at that time. I showed up in the parking lot with a hybrid bike I had borrowed from my mom and a pair of running shorts, tennis shoes, and a tank top. I was mortified to see everyone all decked out in spandex with cycling shoes that clipped into their bikes and fancy bikes with weird handle bars that I had never seen. My first instinct was to let the parking lot clear out, shove my borrowed bike into the car, and never show my face again.

It was at that moment that someone I had met a few days before walked her fancy bike over to my car and told me that she was so glad I was there, and she'd wait for me. I got on my bike and headed out with the group (though far behind). One of the coaches fell back to ride with me and complimented me on how strong I looked on the bike. I'll never forget her words: "You're strong. When you get a better bike, you're going to fly." I went from feeling like I didn't belong to a welcomed part of the group. In the parking lot, I was getting high-fives and was invited to breakfast.

Being a part of that group was a turning point for me. Not only in my journey to become a triathlete, but also in my life. Starting your life over is hard, and it had been a long, lonely winter. I started to feel hopeful again. I gained a community, a new passion, and felt like I moved out of a never-ending transition season into a life that I was excited to live.

Since those days, I've joined many new communities—new gyms, new triathlon clubs, and new teams. Being the new person is never easy. I always experience those same fears and doubts, but I've learned that stepping into the unknown of a new community brings rich experiences and amazing people into my life.

7

COMMON CONCERNS

Am I going to stick out? Look silly? Am I wearing the wrong thing? We all have those questions. Whether it's your first training session or your first race, there are dozens of universal concerns. Here we cover the frequently asked questions at our Triathlon 101 seminars, plus a few you may be afraid to ask.

WILL I LOOK SILLY?

Let's hit the question that everyone wonders about. Yes, you *will* look silly, whether it's from accidentally wearing your wetsuit on the bike, your helmet on the run, or something else. It happens to all of us!

At my first race, I forgot where I racked my bike. Not just for a second either. It was more like three whole minutes, which feels like an eternity during a race. Another athlete in our club, Ron, captured a video of the comedy that ensued. Ultimately, it was a funny story to share later, but at the time it felt humiliating!

Learning to laugh at yourself is the best way to deal with looking silly! Someday, when you're a veteran, your embarrassing moment will turn into a great story to share with tri newbies.

WHAT SHOULD I WEAR?

Let's get one thing out of the way. You don't have to wear a one-piece bathing suit like they do in the Olympics. Theoretically, you can wear whatever you want. When Heather Reynolds started training for triathlon, her biggest concern was tan lines. So she promptly fashioned her tri top into a tube top and wore it that way for years without a second thought. And it worked perfectly fine until the day she realized having pockets would be a huge pro.

In my experience, triathletes worry about what to wear *before* the race, but on the actual day, it's of little concern. Unless, that is, you *really* wear the wrong thing. Then you'll spend the entire race wishing you'd chosen differently!

Ninety percent of athletes at a race will wear a triathlon suit or a tri top and shorts, and your best bet is to do the same. Modern triathlon clothing is moisture-wicking and quick-drying, designed to be worn throughout the entire race. In other words, *you shouldn't change.* Really. There's no place provided for changing—except during a full IRONMAN—and nudity is prohibited.

Shopping for my first race, I didn't believe everyone wore a tri suit. They seemed *so* revealing and unflattering, especially in those dressing room mirrors that highlight everything you want to hide. I was so sure I wouldn't wear one that I bought athletic skirts for the run leg. It wasn't until I got to the actual race and saw all shapes, sizes, and body types—all wearing tri clothes—that I felt better. (I didn't end up wearing the skirt!)

HOW DO I FIND THE RIGHT SIZE?

Unless you're a speed skater or a Cirque du Soleil performer, you're probably not used to wearing clothing as tight as a tri suit. Your mind will say "no way" in the dressing room. Why? The best reason I've come up with is that tri clothes break the universal rule of dressing—pairing a super tight top with a super tight bottom. You *are* supposed to break this rule, just for triathlon.

And your tri suit is indeed supposed to be *tight*. You don't want it causing drag on the bike or swim. So when you're looking in the mirror, wondering if your outfit is too tight, chances are, it's a perfect fit.

WHAT SHOULD I WEAR UNDERNEATH?

Let's talk about undergarments. Wearing a sports bra underneath your tri suit is a *do*—even if it has a built-in bra No matter your chest size, you *need* a bra due to a combination of running, water, and photos. Trust me, you will thank me later when the race photos come out.

And, on the bottom, you wear nothing under your shorts. That's right, nothing at all. Cycling with seams on seams is a high chafing situation. To clarify, both bike shorts and tri shorts are designed to be worn with nothing underneath.

WHAT'S THE DEAL WITH WETSUITS?

Wetsuits provide not only warmth in cool water conditions, but also buoyancy, allowing you to swim faster at a lower heart rate. Age groupers who did not grow up as swimmers typically *love* wetsuit-legal swims because it closes the gap between them and their swim-team peers. Conversely, former competitive swimmers generally *dislike* wetsuits because they confer a greater advantage to adult onset swimmers.

Wetsuit-legal status is based on the water temperature on race morning. Here's the rule per USA Triathlon: "If the water temperature is 78 degrees Fahrenheit or below, then wetsuits are allowed. At 78.1 to 83.9 degrees Fahrenheit, participants may wear a wetsuit at their own discretion; however, wearing a wetsuit in the temperature range will mean that the athletes are ineligible for awards."

Pretty straightforward, right? But when do you *need* a wetsuit? In the upper temperature range of wetsuit optional range (78.1-plus) most participants will feel too warm in a wetsuit. In the lower range, depending on your personal tolerance to cold water, most people are fine swimming without a wetsuit in mid-70s water. Below 72 degrees or so, you really want a wetsuit.

HOW DO I KNOW IF THE RACE WILL BE WETSUIT LEGAL?

This determination won't be made until race morning. Therefore, if you have and hope to wear a wetsuit, a good rule of thumb is to always bring your wetsuit to the race, just in case. Look on the race website, talk to past participants, or read race reports to learn the water temperature in previous years.

DO PEOPLE REALLY PEE IN DURING THE SWIM AND ON THE BIKE?

There may be a day that you'll pee on the bike, but that day should *not* be your first sprint tri. Many athletes racing longer distances like IRONMAN, with a specific time goal in mind (whether it be winning or finishing under the cutoff), *do* pee on their bikes. Nearly all triathletes pee in their wetsuit in the lake. Gross? Yeah, if you think too hard about it. But as I often say, there's a huge difference between what's gross in daily life versus what's gross in a triathlon.

WILL I BE LAST?

Since there can only be one final finisher in any event, you are unlikely to be last. But, if you're last, you'll still have an amazing experience. Triathlon has a culture of celebrating *all* athletes from first to last, and that final finisher will likely receive more cheers than any of the other finishers. If you don't believe me, look up 17-hour IRONMAN finish videos.

WILL THEY LET ME FINISH IF I'M TOO SLOW?

Any sanctioned race should have published cutoffs in their athlete guide. How closely are these cutoffs enforced? It varies. If you're competing in a large national race, like IRONMAN, the posted cutoffs are followed to the minute. However, in my experience, local races are often more flexible with cutoffs. For example, in one popular local Georgia race, a swimmer is allowed to continue as long as they're making forward progress.

SHOULD I BRING MY FAMILY?

Yes. Many local events are hosted at state parks or resorts—family friendly and easy to navigate. And triathletes believe in celebrating afterwards. The atmosphere is festive, often including food, drink, and celebration. Here are a couple of tips to help make spectating easy and fun for your family (so they'll do it again):

» Ask around about spectating spots and tell your crew in advance.

» Consider driving separate cars, especially if there are young kids involved. Can they come late, pick one location to watch, maybe even leave early? Unless they're experienced, you want to *ease* them into popping up in different locations on the course and wearing costumes. That's spectating 201.

» If you're tackling a longer race, like a half or full iron distance, make sure rest breaks are built in. It's tough to maintain cheering momentum from 4AM into the early hours of the next day. A 70.3 or 140.6 can—and usually should—involve a nap/lunch break during the bike leg.

» Race day is all about you. Before and after, do everything you can to keep your spectator happy. Pack them a cooler, promise they can plan the agenda for next weekend, whatever. At the very least, try to make spectating not the absolute worst day of their life.

WILL MY FRIENDS AND FAMILY HAVE FUN SPECTATING A RACE?

We already outlined the basics of spectating. The truth is, for all but the most hardcore fans of the sport, triathlon isn't very exciting to watch. Standing in the hot sun all day to watch your athlete fly by isn't everyone's idea of a good time. Here are some ideas to take spectating to the next level:

» Every race has "hot corners"—the places where everyone wants to stand. But what's more fun and helpful to athletes is to cheer on the more remote parts of the course. That's when racers really need the encouragement! My dad loves doing this, and I recall some rock-bottom times when seeing him in the desert/on the mountain/in the wasteland lifted my spirits. And I enjoy trying to do the same.

» Have a spectating party. My friend Michelle is the queen of costumes and themes for spectating. For some reason, dressing up makes everything more fun.

» Make signs. This is a great way to get kids involved with the day, and the athlete really appreciates it!

Spectating right at IRONMAN Texas 2016

WILL I MAKE A ROOKIE MISTAKE?

The best way to alleviate this fear is to volunteer at a local triathlon where you'll watch race logistics in action. The things that sound complicated now—nutrition, transition, course layout—make more sense when seen in person.

8

TRIATHLON AND BODY IMAGE

Is there any woman alive who hasn't struggled with negative body image? A distorted perception of your shape or a belief that your body size is a personal failing? Maybe you've just felt self-conscious in your own skin. I know I have at many different points in life.

In high school, my pole—for pole vaulting—was rated to a certain weight. We would weigh in before meets, and I was *constantly* flirting with the cutoff number. I tried all the diet pills and was a long-time consumer of ephedrine, now banned.

Then, in college, the combo of stress and the temptation of the unlimited cafeteria plan made things worse. I gained around 20 pounds in a short period of time and was constantly trying fad diets to shed it. None of them worked; when I wasn't eating eight macadamia nut cookies for dinner, I was subsisting solely on SlimFast bars, a habit I perceived as "good." This plan would backfire when, starving after a day of restriction, I would make a midnight run to the local 24-hour Mediterranean fast food joint.

An old roommate and I once made a literal *barrel* of cabbage soup during an ill-fated attempt at a cleanse. It tasted bad and smelled worse. After she caught me cheating with a bag of candy corn two days later, we both bailed. We didn't know what to do with the soup, so we hid it in the guy's dorm, where the smell wafted through for days before they found the source.

During that time, my main motivation was fitting into my cheerleading uniform—plus, I didn't want to be that girl who got bigger every time she went home for visits. I went on crazy diets whenever Christmas break got close. I remember visiting home and telling my friends, "Sorry I can't hang out this break. Because Atkins diet."

After I graduated (and lost the caf plan), things normalized somewhat. But I still had unhealthy habits. In law school, I ate the same thing every day for months—a package of SnackWell's vanilla sandwich cookies in the morning and two of the same sushi roll each night.

When I moved to Fayetteville to be closer to John, things didn't get much better. We fell in with a group who would hang out at the same Italian restaurant from 5PM onward every single night, drinking red wine and eating buttery and bready things for hours.

It was only when I discovered triathlon that things changed for the better. It reinforced a mental shift from food as reward to food as fuel instead. Eat SnackWell's and fast all day? Yeah, your

Ilana Katz, owner of Optimal Nutrition for Life, works primarily with athletes who want to improve their body composition for performance. Here she weighs in on the scope of body image issues:

Negative body image includes both self-criticism and a perception of how others may be "judging." Within my nutrition practice, clients often fall into the trap of worrying about "how they look" versus "how they feel."

The first step toward recovery is to put your body in perspective: instead of obsessing with your "outer" self, focus perceptive attention on what a beautiful machine your body is. It can move, it can hike, it can compete, it can reproduce, it can "placeholder for whatever you love about your life." This is a good start to knowing your own body, accepting it, and celebrating the beauty of YOU.

training session after work will suck. And that bit with the daily Italian feasts? That doesn't bode well for working out that night *or* the next day.

In 2015, when I wanted to maximize body composition for performance without falling into old patterns, I hired Ilana Katz of Optimal Nutrition for Life to help me figure it out. She helped me reach my best performance weight in a healthy way.

Appreciating your body for what it can do, rather than for how it looks, is a lifelong struggle for many of us. In many cases, training for an event *can* help you make that shift. Amy shares how changing her environment and her sport helped change her body image.

AMY'S JOURNEY TO BODY POSITIVE THROUGH RUNNING

Amy Hafner was a dancer her entire life. In college, the environment was competitive—not only in ability but also in terms of dieting and body shape. Many of the women struggled with eating disorders, and it was almost admired, seen as a sign of discipline. "It almost showed that you were serious about things," recalls Amy. "I had a very good friend who was infected with the insidiousness of the message that you should always try to be thinner."

As dance became more about looks versus performance, Amy eventually lost her love for the sport. "I lost the way it made me feel and how I was able to move through space. All of that was lost because it became only about the aesthetic."

After college, Amy searched for a new sport and took a job at a running store. She had grown up running some with her dad and decided to sign up for her first half marathon. At first undereating and not fueling properly limited her performance. She credits her coworkers with helping her see the link between running strong and proper nutrition.

Since making a number of changes, including adding protein and mid-workout fueling to her diet and working on overall strength, Amy has seen her times steadily improve. "I want to keep pushing myself and going after challenging goals."

Every woman has days they feel uncomfortable in their own skin, but when does it move from transient experience to a problem requiring outside intervention? Melissa Smith, an Emory School of Medicine psychiatrist, gives us advice on how to identify disordered eating and when to seek help. Then, two amazing women, Heather Reynolds and Cori James, share their journeys toward improved body image aided by endurance sport.

#TriLessons:
Melissa's Tips to Recognize a Problem

When should an athlete take action if they're concerned about disordered eating? Melissa Smith, an Emory School of Medicine psychiatrist, gives us advice on when to seek help. "If you're having guilt about food, weight, or intrusive and ruminative thoughts, then it's worth a conversation with your doctor or a screening evaluation."

She adds there's no reason to fear a consultation: "Just because you go do an initial evaluation with a therapist doesn't mean you have a major diagnosis. Think of it like a skin check if you have a family history of melanoma. Going to the dermatologist doesn't mean you're going to get skin cancer, but they may be able to find small areas that are concerning and monitor them or treat them before they become a giant problem."

Signs of an Issue
Melissa warns the number one risk factor for an eating disorder is dieting behavior. "If you've ever thought about dieting, if you've ever hidden your dieting under the guise of 'being healthy,' if

you've ever restricted calories, if you've ever avoided 'unhealthy' foods, or if you've ever worked out in order to compensate for what you ate, then you have the number one risk factor for developing an eating disorder."

She also warns that "normal" behavior by society's or sport-specific standards doesn't mean that it's completely benign behavior. For example, purging with laxatives and fluid restrictions are activities endorsed in wrestling. She adds that anyone can be in denial or validate unhealthy behaviors by searching on social media or talking to peers who exhibit similar behaviors. "Anyone can seek out what they're searching for, essentially. So because your friend from high school does x, y, and z, and they seem successful doesn't mean they are healthy, happy, or disclosing all things they are doing."

Say It Out Loud
Being able to press pause on your thoughts and behaviors, take a step back, and look from the outside can be helpful. If you're concerned that a thought/behavior may be unhealthy, then say it out loud (even if you're by yourself). She warns that "if it sounds unhealthy or dangerous out loud, then it probably is. 'I'm going to take laxatives to be one pound lighter' sounds really absurd out loud, yet when it's quietly said inside your mind, it can set off a whole cascade of thoughts that eventually talk yourself into the behavior. Your mind says, 'it's not that big of deal, everyone does it, just this one time.' Write it down if you have to and force yourself to write down risks and benefits under each behavior/thought and then compare. Benefits should always outweigh risks."

Avoid Black and White Thinking

Performance is based on more factors than just calories in and calories out. While focusing on proper fueling is important, it also important to focus on recovery, cross-training/physical therapy to reduce injury, getting sufficient sleep, and hydration status.

"The human body is complex. Appreciating the complexity can help avoid the pitfall of black and white thinking. For example, if you didn't have the best day in regard to nutrition, but you slept well the night before and went to yoga, then you're still successful and moving toward your goals. – Dr. Melissa Smith

Takeaway: Whatever your concerns about your body, know you're not alone. But one amazing tool that sport can give is learning to appreciate your body for what it can do, rather than how it looks.

#TriCourage Story: Triathlon Helped Cori Overcome an Eating Disorder

–By Cori James

There is one special picture that I keep on my phone. It's a picture of my friend and me being silly, our backs turned to the camera, with one hand holding the other's rump. We had just finished a hike with our boyfriends and decided to take a photo to prove to the internet that it had actually happened. I don't keep this picture in my phone library because it's a magical memory or too cute to delete. I keep it because it's the first photo I saw of myself and realized how far I had fallen into the abyss of my eating disorder. The picture was taken from directly behind us so there was no hiding the inches separating my toothpick-sized thighs. Where had my thighs gone?

Cori crossing the finish line of the IRONMAN 70.3 World Championships in 2017

Growing up I was always petite, but my thighs had become friendly with each other. Since early high school, they touched while walking or sitting. Now, at the age of 22, they were these tiny little twigs looking like they were trying to get as far away from each other as possible and could snap at any moment. I stared at this picture in disbelief. "It's not that bad. I'm a runner, so I'm healthy. Thigh gap…this is what I wanted. Thigh gaps are good." Trying to convince yourself that you're not sick is an interesting game.

"I'm a runner, so I'm healthy."

"I'm not in a hospital, so I'm just fine. Girls with eating disorders are hospitalized."

"I haven't lost my period, so nothing is wrong."

This story isn't just about how small I got or the voice telling me I was disgusting even though my body was slowly disappearing in an attempt to appease that voice. This story is about how triathlon helped me overcome a mental illness that was filling my every waking moment with self-hate. During the dark times, as I like to refer to them, I decided that I needed to run at least 6 miles a day while eating about 1,000 calories.

I kept training for races, and in 2014, I trained for my second full marathon. At that point, I was really working to find balance and be healthier. Even though my behaviors were healthier, that voice in my head was still regularly telling me I sucked, and food avoidance was always an option. I was better than the dark times, but I was overtraining and still not eating enough.

After hearing of my issues with food and training, a friend recommended I read a book by the amazing Chrissie Wellington: *A Life Without Limits*. I read this book and absolutely fell in love with triathlon. I swam one year in middle school on a small local team but quit because I thought my teammates were jerks. I had just gotten my first commuter bike the year before, a single-speed Fuji that I had ridden to and from work a number of times, but I had never owned a bike with gears. I was about to run my second marathon, so at least I had some experience there. I wasn't prepared, but I was so ready to take on a new challenge.

There was something different about triathlon that clicked in my brain. I didn't want to be mediocre. I didn't want to do it in the hopes that it would make my body "perfect" or just a way to burn a ton of calories. I wanted to participate in triathlon, and I wanted to be STRONG AND HEALTHY. I don't know why, but my brain flipped that switch and decided it was time to really change. It was when I was able to really become the athlete I had always wanted to be and to stop obsessing over every single bite of food while telling myself I was worthless.

I suddenly stopped craving a smaller body. I craved muscles, strength, and self-confidence. Running had become a means to an end in the past. A way to burn calories and nothing more. It was time to get back to running because I loved it. I was ready to overcome my eating disorder. You know how people always say, "You can't force an addict to quit. They have to make that decision for themselves." I really believe that. I have no idea what it is like to be addicted to drugs or alcohol, but I really was addicted to my eating disorder. I knew it was bad for me and hurting the people who loved me, but it wasn't until that switch flipped and my brain and body took control, that I really knew I could do it this time. I could beat this thing.

Now after three years of participating in triathlon, I can finally say, "I WIN." Not because of some overall podium I might stand on (though that would be pretty kickass), but because I finally beat it. I still have bad days where that voice creeps up to remind me of my past, but now I know how to shut it up. I don't think my eating disorder will ever be 100% gone from my brain, but I know that it will never take over my life again. I owe a lot of that to triathlon and the community that surrounds it. There is no mold for a triathlete to fit into.

At every race, you see folks of all shapes, sizes, colors, genders, and skill levels, but each person that crosses that finish line is treated like a rock star. I've never felt more beautiful than when I'm covered in sweat, running across a finish line with a big ol' smile on my face. Strength is far more important than appearance to me now, and I will forever be grateful for that.

#TriCourage Story: Triathlon Helped Heather Appreciate Her Body

—By Heather Reynolds

I don't know when, how, or why I became obsessed with being thin. I was actually a pretty skinny kid and had a healthy relationship with food growing up. But puberty hit me like a freight train at 14, and I went from being shaped like a cereal box to Jessica Rabbit. A pudgy, confused, very unconfident Jessica Rabbit. And we all know what high school is like, and how catty people can be, and I certainly heard plenty of negative comments.

So I began my first diet, which ended up lasting about 15 years. The summer after my sophomore year, I went about dieting like the overachiever that I was, and I showed that scale who was boss! Within nine months I had lost over 45 pounds, with my weight dipping below 100 pounds. I thought I looked AWESOME. It was the mid-90s—thin was in!

Heather crossing the finish line of IRONMAN Mont-Tremblant in 2015

I was secretly thrilled to have to shop in the kids' section or to have someone comment on how thin I was. But the fun did not last long. My triathlon brain would liken it to reaching the top of a very difficult climb, rejoicing, and then having both tires pop and the wheels fall off as you slowly flop down the back side. I stopped menstruating, which led to doctors' visits, which led to doctors telling me that I had to gain weight, which led to me being depressed, which led to lots of binging and crying and general awfulness.

I won't even begin to try to describe the period that followed because it is very difficult to understand unless you have been there. Even though this is my story, I can barely identify with the feelings I felt back then. How could I not see that I was a good person no matter what body I lived in? No one could have convinced me of that, and as quickly as I was able to transform my body, it would take years and years to transform my mind.

I forged through my senior year of high school, and with my original 45 pounds (plus 10 more for good measure), I started Georgia Tech. I shudder to think of my next five years if I hadn't made the choice to go to this wonderful school. I found the dearest friends of my life here, and I found a self-worth that I had never experienced in my teen years. I was happy, but I can't say that I was completely comfortable in my own skin. Way too much of my time was spent thinking about diets, food, clothes that would make me look thin, how great my life would be if I just was thin, etc.

By the time I left college, I was a very healthy weight, and I took to lots of running and aerobics and gym visits to make sure that it stayed that way. I still have my old day planners where I cataloged each lift, run, class, and crunch. I get bored just thinking about it now.

About nine years ago, two of my girlfriends convinced me to do a triathlon. I trained over the summer to do my first sprint race and had so much fun. The next summer I did more races and continued to enjoy the challenge. The following spring I ran into a guy in Atlanta Cycling who was starting a tri club. Sure, sounds like fun. (Thanks for being there that day, Jim Boylan.)

I did not jump gung ho into the sport as some do. I held on tightly to many of my old tendencies. I rode my bike in a tube top for years, because how was I supposed to look cute in a summer dress with tan lines? And I couldn't quite get behind proper bike nutrition, because I saw that as a wasted opportunity to go into a big calorie deficit and potentially drop weight. But in time, I slowly drank the Kool-Aid. And I made great friends that I looked up to and learned from and wanted to be like.

Triathlon gives many gifts. It gives you discipline—you have to have a training plan and stick to it if you want to do well. It gives you patience—no one can sit on a stationary bike for 2 hours or run for 80 minutes on the Silver Comet without patience. It gives you humility—even the fastest people I know don't always win.

But for me, triathlon has given me an appreciation for these bones, muscles, ligaments, and veins that make up my body. This poor body that I starved, stared at, measured, and judged for so many years has given me the greatest joys of my life in the last few years. It makes me feel strong, and young, and so grateful. It has taken everything that I have thrown at it and surprised me so many times by meeting the challenge. It is a great body, and I am so lucky to have this exact one.

Part Two
Get Prepped

In part one we clarified
your reasons for
participating in triathlon.

Now, it's time to
get everything you
need for training.

We'll discuss gear,
picking a race,
finding time to train,
and setting a
preparation timeline.

GET GEARED UP

As a swim volunteer at the Spring Fling sprint triathlon, my job was to spot swimmers in trouble. After the pack took off, I saw a guy in the rear swimming Tarzan style, sans goggles. "What happened to your goggles?" I asked as he swam past my kayak, thinking he had taken a wayward elbow to the head. "We need GOGGLES for this thing?" he asked incredulously. After I assured him goggles weren't a requirement, he went on to complete the swim, and I assume, the rest of the triathlon. What's the lesson? Though triathlon can be expensive, you don't *need* a lot of fancy, expensive gear to get started. You can do your first triathlon on a shoestring budget. Don't believe me? Let's talk about what you absolutely *need*.

HOW DID YOU COMPLETE YOUR FIRST TRIATHLON ON A BUDGET?

» *"Girls bike, taped old swimsuit to make it black and tight, used foam goggles. Loved every minute of that race!"* –Ryan

» *"I did my first tri using my husband's 1984 Panasonic bike with cages, wore a bathing suit and pulled running shorts over it when I got out of the water, and wore regular running shoes. I basically paid the entry fee only, and I actually placed 1st in my age group!"* – Michele

» *"Borrowed everything! Swam in biker shorts and sports bra! Used every discount code available."* – Tes

TRI-ING ON A BUDGET

After you get hooked on triathlon, go nuts with the latest and greatest gear, budget allowing. But for your first, you're merely trying the sport. Because of that, it makes sense to keep your purchases to a minimum. Here's what you absolutely *need* to get started.

SWIM EQUIPMENT

What you need: Something to cover your body, goggles, a swim cap

When we do a Triathlon 101 session and get to the part about swim equipment, I usually start by saying, "You have to wear... *something.*" Long pause.

For best results, you will want that something to be tight fitting so that it doesn't cause drag. For the ladies, that means a high-necked one-piece, which can be purchased at a local sports store, triathlon shop, or even Amazon. A new suit will run you about $60 to $70. Once you find your size, you can save a lot of money by buying the "grab bag" suits on Amazon. (Note: Expect to get the color combo that no one wanted. I've gotten the orange and brown one three times now.)

Goggles are a necessity. To find the best pair of goggles, I recommend a triathlon shop where they won't mind if you take the goggles out of the package. Stick them to your face, right in the store. If they stick for a few seconds before coming off, then they're likely to also have a good seal in the water. Budget goggles will run you anywhere from $13 to $25.

Finally, unless you have very short hair, you *need* a swim cap. Trust me on this one. Unless you plan to shave your head post swim (due to permanent knots), you need a cap. For open water practice, a bright cap goes a long way toward visibility. This purchase will run you about $5. (Note: Once you start racing, you'll have an endless supply of caps, since they are provided for races.)

BIKE EQUIPMENT

What you need: A bike to use during the race, a helmet, flat kit, and water bottle

The bike is the biggest financial barrier to entry. For a new athlete, it's a huge commitment—a massive outlay of cash for a sport you're not sure you like. That's why I recommend waiting until after your first race to purchase a bike. Why? Well for newbies coming into the sport, what you know on day one and what you *will* know after a few months of training are light years apart. (In other words, you're likely to buy the wrong bike, or the wrong three bikes, like I did.)

For your first sprint tri, train at your local spin class, borrow a bike, or use the old cruiser in the basement. After you get hooked on the sport, you'll have a much better idea of the bike you need. If you absolutely can't borrow one, then you can rent one for around $40 to $100 a day. Keep in mind that try said bike before race day, you'll need to rent it more than once.

You also need a helmet. Know that USA Triathlon rules mandate helmets when you're on your bike before, during, and after the race. An entry-level helmet will run you about $40. Note that a more expensive helmet doesn't mean it protects your head better; it's because of other features like venting, less weight, or cool colors.

It's definitely worth picking up a pair of tri shorts, like we discussed in our common concerns section. An entry-level pair will run you about $50.

You need a water bottle ($5) and a cage ($5-$15) to hold it if you don't already have one. Finally, you need the contents of a flat kit—tire levers (2), a bike pump or CO_2 cartridges, an inflator, a multi-tool, and a spare tube, plus a pouch to hold these items. Your best bet is to go to a local bike shop and ask them to help you assemble a kit. That way they'll make sure you get the right sizes for everything. The contents of the kit will run you about $50.

LEARNING TO CHANGE A TUBE

Learning to change a tube is an important but oft-avoided step before your first race. You do not want to rely on race support. Although they will come to help you—eventually—you could be waiting a long time.

Don't fear it, embrace it!

» Start by asking your local bike shop to demonstrate when you purchase the contents of your flat kit. Be sure to ask about any upcoming tire change seminars. Most bike shops will have them.

» Ask your local tri group or new tri friends to practice with you. If you can't find anyone to help in person, head to YouTube. Seriously. There are thousands of videos that demonstrate step by step.

» Practice. Having someone show you is nice, but nothing replaces learning by doing.

» Practice again. Periodically practice to ensure you keep up your skills.

RUN EQUIPMENT

What you need: Decent, recent pair of shoes

Invest in a good pair of running shoes. That doesn't mean the shoes your friend recommends but the shoes that fit your gait and your unique foot shape. Start at a specialty running store where the experts can evaluate your foot strike and recommend a shoe ($65-$125).

That's it! You now own everything you need to tackle your very first triathlon. Notice we didn't mention Garmins, aero wheels, swimming watches, or buckets. We'll tackle those in our next installment.

ADVANCED GEAR

After you're completely addicted to triathlon, you can invest in some extras. Some of these items can really help you, some are nice to have, and some you don't need at all.

SWIM EXTRAS

Swim equipment extras include things like fins, paddles, a pull buoy, a kickboard, and a band. Hold off on getting these items initially until you know exactly what you'll be using them for. If you end up joining a masters group or taking swim lessons in the future, they will have a specific size of paddle, type of band, and so forth that they recommend.

Bodyglide looks like deodorant and is meant to protect skin against chafing. If wearing a wetsuit, athletes often put Bodyglide on their neck or ankles in order to slide their wetsuit off more easily.

RUN EXTRAS

Many triathletes use Yankz or speed laces, elastic laces that allow you to slide your foot in and out of your shoe easily, thus simplifying and speeding up transition. Many triathletes swear by these laces. Personally (and it depends how your shoes fit and how tightly you tie them), I slide my feet in and out of my shoes with normal laces, leaving them completely tied the entire time.

For training in the heat, you'll want to invest in some moisture-wicking clothing. Seams, cotton, and humidity lead to chafing in all kinds of unexpected places.

This isn't really an extra, but it's important to remember to replace your shoes frequently. Many shoes these days only last 200 to 300 miles, so if you're running regularly, you'll need to replace them several times a year.

GENERAL EXTRAS

A Garmin or other GPS watch is always helpful to have. With the popularity of fitness watches that double as lifestyle watches such as Garmin vivoactive and Apple Watch, you may already have a watch with which you can track your training through an app or online training log.

There is no need to immediately upgrade to the latest and greatest Garmin watch with all the bells and whistles. If you're in the market for a GPS watch, you can usually find last year's model for a very steep discount.

Takeaway: You don't need a ten-thousand-dollar bike or the latest aero gear for your first tri. In fact, our advice is to complete your first tri with minimal cash outlay. Once you inevitably get addicted to the sport, you can invest wisely as you continue to learn about the best purchases for your unique situation.

#TriLessons: Five Tips for Buying a Bike

Enjoying quality time with Bikey, my bike soulmate, during a local sprint tri

Once you get hooked on the sport, it's time for your first big bike purchase. Here are five things I wish I knew that would have saved me a lot of time and money when I was starting out!

1. Get a Bike Fit First.

No really you should. This is actually the most important thing and worth the financial outlay. I can also add my personal story which gives my advice a bit more weight. Long, long ago (nine years ago!), in a land far away (Play It Again Sports in Roswell), I, too, thought a bike fit was unnecessary. I found a bargain, used bike better suited for a 6-foot man (I'm 5'6") and got to work! A week later, I found myself in a parking lot meeting a dude from Craigslist who had a "great deal" on a bike. That one didn't work out so well, either. Ultimately, I went through four, yes FOUR, bikes in the first two years of my triathlon journey. I spent tons of extra money buying special accessories to make my bike work, much more than I would have if I had started with a good fit!

If you're going to buy a bike, look into getting a fit first from a tri shop or bike shop. Many times, if you end up purchasing a bike from that store, then they'll deduct your fit fee. We have a great shop in our area, Podium Multisport, that sells road and tri bikes and delivers on great fits.

2. Buy a Bike Based on Features.

This seems obvious yet, like car shopping, many people make bike purchasing decisions based on appearance or brand perception. I can't count the number of times that I have seen a new athlete post a question like "is such and such a reputable bike brand?" The most important bike feature is fit. After your initial fit, your fitter should give you a list of bike brands with measurements and geometry suited for your body. A sign of a reputable fitter is there should be both brands they sell and those they don't on that list!

Beyond a good fit, there are a slew of features such as components, ability to make fit modifications, and ease of maintenance.

All of these merit consideration prior to something like color scheme entering the mix. The good news is that with the availability of bikes, you should be able to find something that meets your needs and looks great!

3. Don't Necessarily Start With a Road Bike.

Common advice for budding triathletes includes starting out with a road bike. The logic is sound and includes reasons such as a road bike is more versatile, you will use it forever, and you can still ride it if you quit triathlon. But I say it depends on the individual. Some people train awhile and sign up for a season of triathlons prior to ever getting started. If this describes you and you have competitive aspirations, you might as well give yourself every advantage from the start. And if you buy a tri bike instead of a road bike, there's a free speed advantage to the tune of 1 to 2 mph!

One more thing on this topic: Some say that a fast bike is only for "serious" athletes. I would argue the opposite. If your desire is to get to the run leg faster, even if it's just to get it over with, then you can benefit from a fast bike!

4. Keep Searching for the One!

Like the search for the perfect saddle, the search for the perfect bike could take months or years, and you may deal with some lemons along the way. Once I started getting good advice, my bike selections got progressively better till I found my perfect bike, the Felt IA, which I dubbed Bikey. He's speedy, good looking, and he makes me super aero for all the free speed you can buy. He even works (harder) when I'm not in perfect shape. With Bikey in tow, I'm a heck of a lot faster than I would be otherwise even when I'm not setting PRs!

5. Getting Refit.

Yes, we covered this, but the thing about a fit is it doesn't last forever. Our strength and flexibility changes over time as do the types of races we are targeting. It's important to head in for a refit periodically. I recommend getting a refit once per year to make sure you're in your best position whatever your goals may be.

10

RACES AND COACHES

I alluded to the chaotic, out of proper order way in which I attacked triathlon. Nowhere was that more apparent than the way I picked races. I registered for both the Gulf Coast half iron distance and the John Tanner Sprint on December 8, 2008, prior to any of the other steps such as learning about training or purchasing equipment.

Our team races represent varied options so that each person would have at least one that appealed to their preference and schedule. But I thought one was obligated to do as many of the team races as possible. I did 17 races that year, and I'm not sure that included all the run races. Periodization? Training plan? Please. Train as much and as hard as possible was my motto. I'm lucky I didn't get seriously injured that first year. Since I was brand new, the improvement curve was still steep, which only reinforced my longer, faster, harder motto.

Goofing around before the start of IRONMAN Chattanooga 70.3 2017

The following year, I hired a qualified coach who served as my voice of reason in training and in race selection. Fortunately, it's not too late for you to do things right from the start! In this section, we're going to take you step by step through everything you need to pick a race and look at your available training options.

DEFINING TRIATHLON

The usual format for a triathlon today is in the order of swim, bike, and then run, though there are exceptions. If you've ever tried to order the sports opposite, you'll know why.

PICKING YOUR DISTANCE

Most newbie triathletes start with a sprint distance triathlon. A sprint distance isn't standard and normally includes a 400- to 750-yard swim, a 10- to 15-mile bike, and a 5K at the end. Although technically you *can* start with any distance, it's usually a better idea to start with a short race. In recent years, I've seen a trend where many athletes want to skip the shorter distances.

Technically you *could* train for a double IRONMAN for your first event. That doesn't mean it's the best way to progress. Even if your ultimate goal is a longer race, you'll perform better if you work out the kinks and get used to racing by practicing.

Now let's say you're in the opposite situation, and a sprint triathlon sounds too long. There are some options that can make a short triathlon less daunting. You can start with a supersprint triathlon. Like a sprint, the distances aren't standard, but to give an example, a popular supersprint locally is 200 yards swimming, 10 miles cycling, and a 2-mile run.

If the open water swim portion is an issue, you can start with a race that includes a pool swim. These are fairly common and often take place in the start and finish of tri season—early spring or fall when lakes and rivers are cold.

PICKING YOUR TIMEFRAME

In the preface, I quoted our club founder, Jim Boylan, who would open our tri club info sessions with the following: "If you can run or walk a mile, then you're ready to train for a sprint triathlon in 10 to 12 weeks." Having trained hundreds of triathletes directly or indirectly through our tri club, Energy Lab, and corporate programs, I have found this to be true in nearly all cases.

This brings us to our next decision. Just because you *can* train for a sprint tri in 10 weeks doesn't mean that you should wait until a few weeks out to start. The sooner you start, the better off you'll be. In other words, yesterday was the ideal day to begin, but today is the next best option.

Now that doesn't mean you should do *as much as possible* from day one; rather, you can get in the habit of swimming, biking, and running regularly to build up aerobic fitness prior to specific training before the event. If you have a coach individually or as part of a training group, they can best advise you on your "low hanging fruit" or best area of opportunity to pursue before your race-specific plan starts.

If you're brand new to one of the sports, then start learning the skills needed to perform that sport, especially if it's swimming. Above all, you will get in the habit of training in at least one of the sports most days of the week. That way you'll be prepared to maximize the time when your official training plan starts.

HOW MUCH TIME DO I NEED TO TRAIN WEEKLY?

If you allot 30 to 45 minutes per workout, five days a week, you should be able to train for and complete a sprint triathlon.

HOW DO I PICK MY FIRST TRIATHLON?

There are so many races that it can be overwhelming to choose. Plus, there are the factors of race distance or timing which expand or limit the options further. Let's look at some factors to consider:

Distance—You'll have a better experience if you complete a short race first. Practically, you can work out kinks and improve things like transitions. If triathlon performance is important to you, spend time improving at shorter races to best translate the gained speed to longer races in the future. Resist the peer pressure to go too long too soon and give yourself a few years (preferably) to improve.

Timing—Make sure you have enough time to train. A good timeline for a sprint is about 12 to 16 weeks. Could you complete one sooner? If you can swim, there's a good chance you could finish one tomorrow, if forced. But the longer the timeline you give yourself, the more prepared you will be. Conversely, if your timeline is *too* long (like six months away with no intermediate goal), you're likely to get bored and burned out.

Camaraderie—Some may think it's a bad idea to pick a race based on what your friends are doing. Assuming it's an appropriate timeframe and distance, I disagree. It's fun to have your friends cheering you on, and you will enjoy cheering them on as well! In our tri club, we have special target races. You know if you sign up for one you are guaranteed an after-party. If you're not part of a tri club, try putting out an informal poll on Facebook (or ask whoever dragged you into the sport) about the popular races.

PICKING YOUR RACE

Now that you've considered distance, timing, and camaraderie, it's time to actually pick a race. Trifind.com is a great place to start and lists races all over the US. Using the criteria you developed in the last section regarding timing, distance, and camaraderie, you should have a short list of races that could work.

Next, it's time to get more dirt on the possibilities. Each race should have a website that lists tons of helpful information:

» **Course information**—The website will indicate the swim sitch. Is it a pool, lake, or ocean swim? Is the course hilly or flat? Do you have similar terrain on which to train?

» **Water temperature**—The website should list the typical water temperature and whether the race has been wetsuit legal in the past. If the race *is* wetsuit legal, do you want to deal with the added complication of procuring a wetsuit? Note: Your training pool is probably 78 to 82 degrees and below mid-70s is the point where you'll really want to wear a wetsuit.

» **Beginner friendly**—Are there clues to indicate whether the course is beginner friendly or not?

» **Race reports**—Look up the name of the race + "race reports." Unless the race just started, there should be a plethora of information available.

» **Ask around**—Ask your friends about the race. Is it suitable for a first-timer? Is the course technical? Are there enough aid stations?

» **Email the race director**—Consider emailing the race director with your questions.

COACHING OPTIONS

Should you hire a coach? Contrary to what many believe, a coach is not only for advanced athletes or someone whose primary motivation is performance. The benefit of getting a coach at all levels is that you can outsource a lot of the things you would need to learn on your own. Instead of learning the hard way that, say, you should get a bike fit before buying a bike, you can have someone tell you things like that.

They can also help you be more efficient with your time and money. I've worked with many athletes who need to make their training time as efficient as possible. For example, if you work a busy job, have kids, and want to complete an IRONMAN, you have little time to waste making mistakes in training. You need to streamline your efforts while also having the confidence you've done the right training to successfully cross the finish line.

Let's say you've decided to take the plunge and look for a coach. Ideally you should interview several. As you speak with different coaches, keep in mind that a very important element is personality fit. Every coach should "meet the client where they are" to some degree; however, you, as a client, may be looking for different amounts of accountability, technical knowhow, and nurturing, etc.

One piece of information you should share with potential coaches is your "driving why," which we talked about in an earlier chapter. Is your main motive social, competitive (with oneself or others), or something else? Is the social, in-person aspect important to you, or is coaching more of a logical process? The analytical coach focused on performance may not be the best fit for a newbie athlete aiming to cross their first sprint finish line. Here are some of the coaching options you will see.

In-person coach—An in-person coach is someone you may see at training sessions or who may occasionally train alongside you. It's someone you can look in the eye when you tell them about your goals, wins, and areas of improvement. An in-person coach works well for someone who is motivated by social reasons.

Online coach—An online coach can be just as helpful depending on your needs. If you're the type of person who is busy, travels, has a young family, and basically needs to wring every bit of value out of every second of the day, then an online coach may be for you.

Deirdre, who shared her story earlier, is an athlete I've coached remotely through the popular software TrainingPeaks. Her situation is a little different in that she *was* local, but we maintained coaching when she moved. Deirdre has noticed some benefits to online coaching. "Everything is available instantly, and it helps you stay organized. Yes, you do miss the one-on-one interaction, but you have now a bigger pool of coaches you can choose from."

Hybrid options—Check to see if there are hybrid options in your community. In ours, we've offered an option that is a mixture of coaching and group training. The athlete receives a plan specific to their race along with group interaction and coach support.

Triathlon clubs—I have mentioned tri clubs in passing several times, but I cannot say enough about how wonderful they can be. Social support and the practical matter of having friends who'd rather meet you at a bike ride than happy hour (or at least meet you at happy hour *after* a bike ride) will go a long way toward your enjoyment and longevity in the sport. If you're not sure about the coaching option, then joining a tri club is also a great way to gain access to local coaches.

ARE YOU COACHABLE?

In my experience, coachable athletes have several things in common. They all have a strong desire to improve, and they aren't sure of their limits. Instead of adhering to a rigorous high bar that may or may not be feasible, they accept that nothing is certain and are willing to work hard and see where they land. They are happy with their progress but never satisfied because there is always more to improve. The coach–athlete relationship goes both ways, too. Over the years, athletes have inspired me to strive to be better, be more committed, and be kinder to myself.

Takeaway: Signing up for a race is a great way to keep on task and amp up the excitement as you prepare to start training. Resist the temptation to "go big" by signing up for a really long or epic race for your first. While you're researching various race options, look into local training groups or coaches.

Next, my friend and athlete, Meg Geshay, shares her reservations about coaching and how her mind was changed.

#TriCourage Story: Meg's Experience Being Coached at Age 40+

–By Meg Geshay

Meg and me before tackling a local sprint tri

Confession: I may be a "little" stubborn. What I mean when I say "little" is probably more like the equivalent stubbornness level of a team of pack mules. I'm being honest. Just ask my husband. I tend to get stuck on an idea or thought pattern, and it takes an act of congress to change my mind. Typically, I am able to disguise the depth of my "stuck" to friends and acquaintances by *clever* maneuvers such as avoidance and, well, avoidance.

Fortunately, through perfecting the art of avoidance, I have reached an age north of 40 in which I rarely have to deal with confrontation (except, of course with family, but that is for a different medium in which to share possibly, never; see, I did it again…avoid! avoid! avoid!). Therefore, as a stubborn older-than-40 lady, I was one of the last people to engage the help of a triathlon coach. I am sharing my experience because I have had my views profoundly changed through this endeavor. I also feel like I've been blessed with a great coaching relationship and feel strongly that is the way it should be.

Initially, a dear friend of mine introduced me to the exceptionally foreign idea of having a coach. She and her husband have been professionally coached, extremely skilled, age-group triathletes as long as we have been friends. This friend also was my running partner for almost two years before she even suggested I consider hiring a coach. Clearly, she knew what she was dealing with in this mule! But, as a true friend will do, she spoke truth to me. She told me I wasn't getting any younger (thank you!), and if I wanted to try for a marathon PR after the age of 40, I needed to do something different than what I had been doing for 20-plus years. I was shocked and quickly thought of about 100 valid reasons why I am not well-suited for hiring a coach. The list of DON'T DO ITs in my head was very long, but I will share with you the top few biggies, and how my mule brain has changed.

1. Mule brain says, "I am so-very-NOT talented enough of a runner to have a coach!" I thought coaches were for really fast and talented people—maybe former collegiate athletes or people trying to go "pro" and win money. They are the elite peeps who have coaches. Not people like me! I am a stay home mom! I've been blessed to enjoy and be healthy enough to run

consistently and recreationally since I was 18 years old. Due to my constitution (see above "stubbornness"), I have been able to adequately train for and complete several marathons and half marathons over the last two decades, but certainly have never considered myself competitive.

While I dreamed of getting faster, logging more miles, and hitting PRs, the reading and research I had done on my own seemed to have tapped me out skill-wise. I felt like I knew what I was doing, but my body just wasn't born to move faster. Why on earth would a coach want a slow nobody like me? Well, pleasantly I have completely changed my attitudes regarding "talent" level and coaching. I have realized, it is about chasing *my* dreams and tackling *my* obstacles. It's not about what anybody else is doing or how fast they are doing it. I understand now that coaching helps me to define and meet my goals which at times may be a number on a race clock. But also, maybe I'm finally growing up, but I have realized that my "training" goals have much more to do with relationships, health, and balance than race results.

Talent or not, I know that my goals are from the heart. What gets my mojo going and excites me? My coach has helped me figure that out. Also, those goals are a moving target, which is a reality of life. I get so excited thinking about what's next, but really, the excitement is about who I am sharing that with. That is my real training goal AND a life goal…they're one in the same for me.

2. My mule brain says, "You really want to be responsible for disappointing someone else?" I have people in my life that I exhaust myself in attempt to not disappoint. By choice I figuratively dance, scramble, sing, and jump to please these loved ones. Truthfully, I think that is the makeup of the fabric that is

me. For the most part, I am a pleaser. I like doing for others. The idea of paying someone to worry about whether they are going to be happy with me and my accomplishments terrified me. The coaching relationship had to be established and experienced for a few months for me to understand and trust that is not going to happen. Granted, I am blessed with a super amazing coach! However, she has taught me through her words and actions her "disappointment" is not part of the equation of our relationship. While I fully believe she is supporting me to reach my goals, if and when I do not, the conversation never has a punishing or negative tone. In fact, I feel like I have a clean slate to start with each day—like, what do I get to do today? What I also appreciate is that her words and actions are not empty sunshine blowing, as that would be exhausting, too! It is something you have to experience, I think, to understand, but it has everything to do with trust. Yes, I still disappoint myself (almost daily), but I have never worried about disappointing her with my "performance" or lack thereof in either training or racing. If you are like me, triathlon is your outlet, hobby, fun. and entertainment. There is no room in your hobby to accommodate someone else's disappointment. I'm way too hard on myself to pay someone else to be also!

3. My mule brain says, "Wait, this is too much money to spend on myself!" Yes, it is a financial investment. My hubby and I try to be fiscally responsible, and hiring a coach seemed frivolous. Fortunately, we were able to make room in the family budget for me to commit for one whole year. I do think that was an important timeframe in order to see if coaching gave me "results." HA!

What I did not realize is how much more I have gained from having a coach than faster split times. Life enrichment with a new network of friends, experiences, training locations, social opportunities, training partners, community outreach…the list is lengthy. I cannot put a price tag on the blessings my family and I have received through this new outlet. I have heard athletes jokingly say, "coaching is cheaper than therapy." I will repeat that without the sarcasm, because honestly, I have done both. Hands down, for me, having a coach is exponentially better than therapy. I am NOT discounting a real need for psychotherapy at times in people's lives (I have a master's degree in counseling and practiced for several years as a therapist before having kids). I am just saying that, for me, at this point in my life, not being in therapy but having a successful coaching relationship is working. And, it is cheaper. I call that winning.

If you feel like you may want to take the leap and hire a coach, but have been on the fence, know that it is way more than having a plan in training peaks laid out for you. I will say again that I am blessed with an exceptional coaching relationship; however, I think that should be the norm. Unfortunately, I believe there are a lot of not-so-great coaches out there with their own agendas. Take your time and find the right one for you. Trust your gut. You will know pretty quickly if you can work well with someone.

Along with my coach, I also feel I get the privy of accessing her team of coaches who are just a fun, easy knowledgeable group that enjoy helping athletes be their best. They are generous with information and time. Additionally, they have welcomed my stubborn and challenging attitude. My "whys?" regarding training always get answered fully and with a depth that helps me learn. Take it from this mule, don't let stubbornness get in the way. Let it work for you.

11

MAKING SPACE TO TRAIN

I nodded like a bobble-head doll while my coworker talked *at* me. She was describing—in detail—the weeks of research involved in purchasing kitchen tile. I couldn't focus on details beyond that it sounded so time consuming and expensive. Also, boring. "How can she possibly have time for all that?" I thought, making the judgment without even realizing that's what I was doing.

Then the conversation turned to me. "What are *you* doing this weekend?" another coworker asked. I demurred at first saying I wasn't sure. "Perhaps a little bike riding," I added, thinking of my plan to tally a solid six hours over the weekend in prep for my upcoming IRONMAN.

There was no way I would share my real plans. But why? It wasn't until later I realized the truth. Just as I judged my coworker for "wasting her time" obsessing about kitchen tile, she was likely to have made the same judgment right back at me. Just as I was thinking "who possibly has time for all that," she was likely to think—or say—the same thing.

The lesson: Neither of us *had* time for the other's hobby, but we both *made* time for our own interests. Beyond the necessities like work, family, and school, we all have *some* choice with how we spend our remaining time, even if the time left is minimal. In this chapter, we discuss creative strategies for time management no matter your situation.

HOW I MAKE TIME TO TRAIN

Time is an extremely valuable resource, especially when you're adding an activity that has the potential to be quite time consuming. There are certain tasks in life that can't be hacked. But for most everything, there are ways to increase your efficiency, and thus your available time. Here are a few strategies I use regularly.

Batch everything—There's nothing as frustrating as a meeting on one side of town, then a two-hour break with just enough time to run home and check email, then another drive elsewhere to an appointment. Before you know it, your day is filled with a couple of hours of productive tasks that suck up all the hours. Because of this principle, I stack appointments whenever possible by side of town. And I try to put as many as I can on one or two days of the week and preserve the rest. If there are breaks in between, I fill them in with phone meetings and bring my laptop everywhere so I'm always ready to get things done during any wait.

Use technology—In some situations, in-person meetings are necessary. But in all the others, I try to use technology to save time—phone, text, Skype for video options. If my physical presence doesn't add value, then I won't be there. I used to feel like I had to come up with a good explanation. Now I just inform someone politely that I need to call in.

When Kathryn and I record podcasts for *Grit and Dirt* (www. gritanddirt.com), we're rarely in the same location. Instead we use Zencastr (a recording software) and type back and forth on a Google doc during the call so we can organize who speaks next. I've scheduled doctor's appointments this way, too. Some visits need to be in person, but simple 10-minute discussions with a physician are more easily accomplished by phone.

Train from home—Group workouts are great for social reasons, but when time is tight, there's nothing like jumping on your already setup bike and knocking out a one-hour workout in one actual hour. Each week I plan a few group workouts so I can see friends or get that extra motivation boost. The rest I organize with the goal of efficiency.

Get rid of errands—Going to the pharmacy, the grocery store, or the dry cleaners are all things I've mostly dropped. Amazon will deliver nearly anything needed within two hours to many locations. Mail-order prescriptions are a great way to save a trip to the pharmacy.

Outsource things—Budget allowing, lawn care and house-cleaning are also good things to outsource. Using a resource like Thumbtack, I've found people to perform other important but non-urgent, time-consuming tasks like picking up junk or steam cleaning the carpets. If you're so inclined, outsourcing meal prep is another great timesaver.

Streamline getting ready—Cut down on grooming time by embracing the locker room. Once upon a time, I hated showering at the gym. Now that I'm used to it, I enjoy it because it's quick and easy. Get some flip flops and get over it. In the same vein, a makeup routine can take less than five minutes. For long hair, a bit of dry shampoo and a bun saves time after workouts. A workout tank or running tights serves as a great base layer for a work outfit so you can avoid changing later.

Be prepared with gear—There's a good reason to have all the things for training available in your car: swim gear, bike gear, and run gear. An extra work-appropriate outfit also comes in handy for the days you forget a key piece.

Meal prep—Figure out a way to streamline your meal prep. Some people do this by making food for the week on a weekend day or freezing food for later. There is a myriad of meal delivery services that come as assemble-your-own (like HelloFresh) or pre-made meals (like Freshly). John and I have groceries delivered twice per week, and the evening meal is usually as simple as a meat plus a vegetable. I am no chef, and I dislike cooking, so when it's my turn to make dinner, I stick to a few easy basics. I can whip up the following simple meals in 10 to 15 minutes of prep plus cook time:

» Chicken thighs plus sweet potato fries

» Taco salad—everything you want in a taco minus the tortilla

» Steak and Brussel sprouts

» Crockpot barbeque chicken plus baked beans

Multitask smart—Bread-and-butter runs for me are usually with dogs in tow while I catch up with podcasts at 1.5 speed. (Note: This doesn't work as well if you're doing intervals!) I reserve long car rides for phone catchups.

Hopefully this list of ways I manage my time has got you brainstorming about how to best find time in your own schedule.

Here are some ways others save time:

» *"I set the alarm on my phone for the time I'm willing to spend on a given activity. When the alarm goes off, I change to the next activity—no exceptions."* –Nicole

» *"I use my Amazon Echo smart thingy and ask it questions about my calendar, the weather, etc. when I'm getting ready in the morning. It makes my coffee and can turn on appliances, too. If only I could figure out how to get it to upload my training!"* –Dani

» *"Before I go to bed, I write down three things I have to do the next day in order to feel accomplished. Those are my non-negotiables."* – Marjan

STEPS TO FINDING TIME

What can you cut? If you're like most busy people, you're using your available hours, you don't just "have" extra to spare. Ditch something you're already doing to make room for this new level of activity. Here are a few ways to do that:

» Make a list of your non-negotiable activities for a week. For example, you can't drop eating, sleeping, getting kids ready for school, family time, or work. Count up the hours all that takes.

» Make a list of the ways you spend your time on things you do that aren't non- negotiables such as watching TV, going to happy hour, surfing on your phone. Count up those hours.

» Make a list of things on list one that could be done more efficiently and how. For example, if you can't figure out how to get in training due to lack of childcare, perhaps you can trade off with a neighbor or trade off weekend mornings with your spouse. He gets an hour while you watch all the kids then switch. PS...if a gym membership is a possibility for you then join one with childcare.

» See where you're willing to cut and where you're not. Everyone has different time management challenges. It is duly noted that kids add a whole new time challenge variable to the mix.

» Whether your biggest limiter is time, money, or a combination of both, try to find shortcuts to make things possible for you.

» Think of ways you can incorporate training into your life. For example, if you work in a high rise, you may sub walking up 15 flights of stairs for your workout in a pinch.

» Consider instituting a rule that you can't "add" anything to life without taking something else away.

LEARNING TO SAY NO

As someone who chronically said "yes," I had to learn how to say "no." Here was the issue: I'd say yes to nearly everything with good intentions, yet it would leave me resentful and burned out, unable to enjoy the things I actually *did* want to do.

There are good things in life and there are great things. Too much in the first category can supplant activities in the second. You should be able to say no without consequence and without explanation. If you have trouble saying no, then try these steps:

» Thank the person for the opportunity.

» If you're not sure, then tell them you'll get back to them in a few days.

» Consider a compromise. If leading the committee isn't the right decision, offer to stay connected in a way that works for you.

» Separate rejection and refusal. Saying no doesn't mean you're rejecting the person.

» Feel good about your decision.

GETTING UP EARLY

Fitting training into your schedule often involves early mornings. If you're not naturally a morning person, making the transition can be tough. Here are some of the responses I've heard from others and in my own head:

» "Training in the morning is hard!"

» "I'm not a morning person!"

Very few people are stoked the moment their alarm goes off. Realizing this fact lets you off the hook. I like knowing that very few people jump out of bed excited to face the day at 4AM. It means you can do it anyway even if you "hate getting up early." It means you don't have to wait until it sounds like a fun prospect, because it's likely that day will never come. "I didn't have the motivation" isn't a good excuse. If it was, many people wouldn't pay bills, do chores, or go to work.

Working as a personal trainer then running a cycling studio for years, I frequently got up early but never enjoyed it until recently. Sure, I liked how much I could accomplish when I did get up early. I loved that it made me feel "ahead," and the security that my activity, whatever it was, wouldn't be supplanted by obligations later in the day. But that didn't mean I was ecstatic when the alarm went off!

Bottom line, it's okay if you're missing the gene that enables you to be as peppy as a modern-day Richard Simmons at 6AM. Since a warm bed will *always* sound better at the time than getting up to exercise, let's explore some ways to set ourselves up for success instead.

EARLY MORNING MOTIVATION

Want to know how other morning exercisers make it happen? I asked some of our 6AM cycling instructors at Energy Lab for their best tips. Some of these folks have dutifully been attending 5:30 and 6AM classes for as long as we've been open!

"Sleeping in workout clothes, setting alarm away from bed, coffee brewing, meeting an accountability partner." – Carolina

"Join Classpass, where they charge you $20 if you miss a class." – Heather

"Visualize a fitter, faster, happier self. I know that after my workout I'll be pumped and feel great the rest of the day!" – Tim

"Put the alarm clock away from the bed; allow for time to wake up and drink coffee." – Ted

"Eating helps shift your sleep cycle. So if you eat in the morning when you wake up, your body will start to expect it...and it wakes up earlier." – Ed

"Have a morning workout in Training Peaks. The power of green. I also found an alarm app that requires you to do a math problem or solve a puzzle before you can turn it off; kind of ridiculous and annoying but also kind of genius." – Michelle

The most creative ideas came from instructor Sara, who offers several suggestions:

"Think about the breakfast you get to have after. Become a coach; you can't slack when you have to unlock the doors. Move an hour away so you have a long drive to "wake up." Eat chips and wine for dinner so you feel guilty enough to drag your butt up or your clothes won't fit. Know that if you don't, your day will probably turn to xxx and your hopes of an evening workout goes out the window (see: chips and wine). Or remind yourself how GREAT it feels to show up for the rest of your day already accomplished with a clear head and full of crazy workout energy."

PLAN TO SUCCEED WITH A BEDTIME ROUTINE

A successful early morning workout requires planning the night before. Here are some ways to set yourself up for success:

» **Lay out everything you will need in the morning**—If you're running, find your running shoes and your (charged) watch. For swimming, have everything laid out plus something warm to wear to the pool. For extra credit, wear your workout clothes to bed!

» **Set up equipment**—If you're cycling, set your bike up on the trainer, or lay out your equipment for an outdoor ride.

» **Driving and traffic plans**—If your plans involve driving somewhere to work out, then plan traffic patterns accordingly. For instance, one athlete saved a lot of time by training near work, knocking out the commute before rush hour. Instead of getting up, prepping for a workout, training, showering, then driving to work, he saved nearly 30 minutes of commute and

15 minutes of prep time this way and used the drive time to "prep" with coffee and breakfast.

Takeaway: There are areas in life you can't cut back—your job, your commute, sleeping, taking care of kids and pets, and working. However, there are likely other things you can cut back on, delegate, say no to, or outsource.

#TriLessons: Stay in the Crosswalk

"I tell you not to worry about your life! Don't worry about having something to eat or wear. Life is more than food or clothing. Look at the crows! They don't plant or harvest, and they don't have storehouses or barns. But God takes care of them. You are much more important than any birds. Can worry make you live longer? If you don't have power over small things, why worry about everything else? – Luke 12:22-26

I learned one thing from my brief stint in law school, and it can be summed in four words: stay in the crosswalk. In the original context, it had something to do with torts, negligence, and what to do if you're a pedestrian getting hit by a car.

Stay in the crosswalk. My torts professor was not suggesting we vault the car in an insane parkour move or stop it with telekinesis—both improbable scenarios. Instead, he charged us with one simple piece of a much larger chain of events—the only thing we could control. This lesson stuck with me, but the phrase itself has come to mean much more.

In 2010, John and I took on our first 140.6 at IRONMAN Wisconsin. We had no idea how to train, and somewhere we got the advice to do as many centuries as possible and run as many 20-milers as we could survive. Wanting to give it my best effort, my training was *all* "hard" and *no* "smart." A three-hour run in the mountains while traveling for a wedding with three hours sleep? No problem. Century rides that involved heat exhaustion and crying? Part of the experience! Basically, I ran myself completely into the ground. When I finally did arrive at the starting line, my last two weeks of training consisted of physical therapy, chiropractic care, and little else.

An IRONMAN Wisconsin swim tradition is to yell "moo" when you round the swim buoys. I knew that going into the race, but I was so frantic—hyperventilating so hard—during the swim I remember thinking, *"how can they be yelling moo when we're all about to die?"* I was absolutely floored to make it out of the lake alive, and then it was onto the bike.

I wasn't prepared there either. I rode an ill-fitting, too-large bike (that was a great deal!) with an equally terrible bike fit (lots of self-adjustment) and a torture device of a saddle. To compound the situation, I skipped pumping my tires because I felt superstitious about flats. What commenced was one of the most painful bike rides of my life. By mile 40, I couldn't get in aero. By mile 80, I couldn't sit. I had to stand at every minor crack or bump in the road because of excruciating saddle pain. And during the run my calf (still residually injured from my first marathon) acted up, so I had to run alongside the road in soft grass.

I could have quit and justified it easily dozens of times. The only reason I didn't was a combination of good old-fashioned pride and staying in the crosswalk. To only think about one more swim stroke, enduring five more miles on the bike, and jogging to the next aid station.

Wisconsin was extraordinarily painful, but it's also now one of my best tri memories.

Find the actions you control and do them. Sometimes that's all you *can* do. If you repeat the pattern that leads to success, then your efforts, in many cases, eventually pay off. Some days training won't go as planned, and others it won't happen at all. Sometimes "life" will interfere, and your best efforts won't be enough. All you can do is set yourself up the best you can. In the previous chapter and the one that follows, our focus is on something that sounds easy, yet is extraordinarily difficult. Here are a few tips that help me stay in the crosswalk:

Be kind to yourself—Have you ever beat yourself up at the end of the day for not accomplishing as much as you "should?" I know I have! For me it helps to pretend someone else is telling me all the things they did. When I consider it from that angle, I am often impressed with "their" efforts instead of disappointed in what I never got to.

But don't give up too easily—"I tried to get up early and it didn't work." "I set the alarm clock, and when it went off, I turned it off." We've all made excuses like these, but does it really count as trying?

Keep trying—Did injury or illness set you back? Is the race you originally planned too far out of reach? Try to think of the long game. Perhaps instead of a spring race, you should consider a fall one. Perhaps instead of an Olympic tri, a sprint is better to start with.

12

PREPARATION GOALS

"Prepare for everything you can control," they said. "Focus only on your preparation." This is advice that's easy to say but hard to follow. Most of us are guilty of one extreme or another. Either we're overly optimistic, making high bar goals which partly depend on things we can't control, or we wing it, leaving too much to chance and failing to fully prepare. Because if you don't have a goal then you can't be disappointed. Am I right?

For my first long race, the Gulf Coast Triathlon, I went way too hard on the high goal side. I thought I was going to kill it, when the truth was I went a little light on the preparation. First off, I had no idea what I was in for. I had done pretty well at my first sprint the previous month, the John Tanner Sprint, and I completed two rides over 40 miles after that, so I figured I was set.

In transition on race morning, I realized how much better I could have prepared. The other athletes looked so "professional"—tan, shaved, lean—just like my imagined version of a triathlete. They looked purposeful in transition, too. Meanwhile, I stood around staring at everyone like some sort of stalker. Maybe I'd pick up a trick or two that would make all the difference?

Next up was wrestling on my wetsuit, a closeout special I'd found at a tri expo for only $50 (yet another unresearched buying decision). I was pretty proud of my purchase. It was such a good deal! *But*...it was sized for someone six inches shorter and 25 pounds lighter. So wrestling that thing on took some doing, and practically a whole can of PAM. Twenty minutes later, I squeezed into it. I smelled like a buttered turkey, and I couldn't stand up straight because of my tightly bound shoulders.

While waiting to start, I checked out the ocean situation. It looked like a scene out of *The Perfect Storm*. I could tell both John and my mother-in-law were concerned for my safety. My wonderful mother-in-law even shed a few tears! And she wasn't the only one. There was a girl on my team, an experienced IRONMAN finisher, crying with fear from the choppy conditions, and I was the one comforting her! What in the world had I gotten myself into? It was only good old-fashioned pride that kept me from bailing.

When the gun went off I wished I had spent more time in open water or tried a practice swim in the ocean. Surely there was a knack for getting past the breakers that pounded me backwards over and over? I was elated when I came out of the swim alive.

On the bike I finally acknowledged my limiter in previous long rides, excruciating full-body pain—the product of an ill-fitting bike, bad saddle, and no bike fit. It turns out there was a reason I never made it past 40 miles in training. I made it through—

barely— and was excited to hit the run, where I was sure I would crush it. Alas, the lack of bike training also affected my run. Who knew!

Needless to say, when I did finish the race, I had a greater respect for the distance and many ideas for improvement. Looking back at my naiveté, there were a lot of things out of my control. It would have been hard to mimic the coastal wind conditions. Certainly, it would have been impractical to hit the beach every weekend for ocean swim practice. But the place I had failed was controlling the variables that I could control. Namely, my own preparation.

For your very first race, I'd encourage you to set benchmarks for preparation, focusing on controlling only what you can control. That sounds like an easy task, yet it can get confusing, as many goals are a mixture of things you can control and others you can't.

For this section, we enlisted the help of a goal-setting expert, certified mental performance consultant, Abby Keenan. Abby's helped first-time athletes and Olympic Trials qualifiers set and achieve appropriate goals.

YOUR PREPARATION

Starting where you are includes assessing where you are and comparing where you want to be in the future. Abby suggests strengthening your commitment to your goal by selecting one that's feasible to achieve. For example, if you swam in high school and participate in all three sports regularly, it's well within your reach to finish a sprint triathlon in a few months. Conversely, if you don't run at all, maybe the goal for those first 12 weeks is to progress to running 30 minutes straight. Or if you have a fear of deep water, perhaps your 12-week goal would be to swim a certain distance, proficiently and confidently, in the pool.

When you're excited about a goal, it's natural to want to conquer it immediately. Trust me, I might be the most impatient person on the planet. Yet, in triathlon, as in most things, there's no rush. Triathlon will always be there, so don't let yourself be hurried by an ill-advised preparation timeline.

By this point, you probably have some ideas on goals and the timeline involved. If so, think about what could potentially stand in the way of achieving your goals. Time? Money? A frequently changing work schedule? Keep these things in mind as you're building your timeline and choosing focus areas.

DETERMINE FOCUS AREA

Your focus area could be many different aspects of a run or tri event. For example, maybe you've run in the past but haven't run regularly in years. Your focus area could be building your run durability and increasing your resilience to injury by increasing your mileage and frequency slowly. Or if you're a fearful swimmer, your focus should be increasing confidence and proficiency swimming indoors before venturing to the lake. Don't make the mistake of trying to focus on everything; pick the areas where you need the most work.

Example One: When I signed up for my first 70.3, a race approximately six months out, I could only swim a continuous

50 yards without stopping to rest. Therefore, I had a lot of steps between that and being 1.2-mile ocean swim ready. Since you have to finish the swim to complete the race, this was a needed area of focus.

Example Two: Lindsay signed up for a sprint tri in six months, but she didn't know how to swim at all, and she has a fear of deep water. Therefore, she must factor swimming confidently and safely into her timeline as well as being race ready.

BACKWARDS PLAN AND CHECKPOINTS

Having a huge goal that's extremely far away can be tough without milestones along the way. For example, the popularity of some races, like many IRONMAN races, necessitate signing up a whole year ahead of time! Yet I cringe when I see someone start their countdown to a race a whole year out. "Only 360 days to go, I better get to the pool!" Instead of having one giant goal too far away to motivate, set up intermediate goals along the way.

Next, start at the deadline and work backwards to see what you need to achieve, noting shorter term checkpoints to keep you on track. If your big goal is to do an Olympic-distance triathlon, for example, you'll want to complete a sprint triathlon first. And to complete a sprint triathlon, you'll have to make sure you allow yourself time to train, find an event, and purchase the necessary equipment.

Example One: I signed up for a May 70.3 (Gulf Coast) in December of 2008, giving me six months to train. To stay on track, I signed up for a sprint-distance triathlon in late April. Prior to the sprint, I planned to get in four open water swims. And prior to my first open water swim, I expected to work up to one mile in the pool. Prior to my 70.3, I wanted to complete the full 70.3 distance in the pool.

Example Two: Lindsay, our hypothetical swimmer, has a sprint triathlon in six months. Working backwards, she'll give herself three months devoted to specific training for her race. The three months prior to that will be dedicated to increasing her confidence and competence in the water.

FOCUS AREAS

Within the focus areas you outlined, determine process goals for each. Abby describes these as daily or weekly actions that work toward your checkpoints and long-term goal. "It's very important to state these positively instead of negatively. An example process goal would be to run three times per week or to practice swim drills two times per week. A negatively phrased goal would read "don't eat junk food.""

Example One: Focus Area, Backwards Plan, and Checkpoints

» In order to improve my technique, I vowed to take two swim lessons and practice three times per week at the pool from January until race day.

» Before the 70.3, I wanted to complete a 2,000-yard pool swim by the end of April.

» To gain experience racing, I planned a sprint triathlon (600-yard swim) at the end of April.

» In order to safely complete those swims, I vowed to complete a 2,000-yard pool swim in three months and practice in open water four times prior to race day.

Example Two:

» In order to improve her form and endurance, Lindsay signs up for a one-on-one swim lesson and a group swimming class.

» She commits to practicing three times a week whenever possible from now until race day in order to reinforce and improve her skills.

» She shares her goals with friends, family, and her new swim coach. Her swim coach will serve as the expert to make sure her goals are realistic and to keep her on track.

CELEBRATE THE WINS

Last year, my husband's business coach encouraged him to begin celebrating wins both big and small. It's a simple action we've found leads to more positivity in general. It's all too easy to dwell on the things that go wrong instead of right. It's something we've done together ever since. It doesn't mean we're pulling out the balloons and cake every day; rather, we're simply verbally expressing or writing down small successes.

At first, I discovered my definition of a "win" was too stringent. Writing 1,000 words didn't feel like a win when I wanted to write 3,000. Getting in 20 minutes of jogging wasn't satisfying when I hoped to achieve 45.

Eventually, I realized my expectations were interfering with recognizing my accomplishments. I was putting crazy pressure on myself and was not happy unless I hit an arbitrary high-bar goal. In contrast, celebrating the small wins necessitates being kinder to yourself—something that's easy to say but challenging to do.

It is possible to be happy but not satisfied. I encourage you, from the beginning of your endurance sports journey, to start recognizing wins both big AND small.

Takeaway: Get in the habit of celebrating wins daily, whether it's sharing them with accountability partners, journaling, or something else. If you're setting yourself up for success with mini-goals and checkpoints, you should be experiencing wins on a regular basis. Got up and made it to the pool this morning (even if your swim wasn't awesome)? That's a win! Got in *a* workout, even if it was interrupted midway by a call from your boss? That's a win, too.

#TriLessons: When Preparation Doesn't Happen

In October 2012, I toed the line of IRONMAN Hawaii in Kona, a long-time dream. I was prepared...ish. I was ready to take on the day...in a manner of speaking. Yet, on the day, I very nearly didn't finish at all.

That summer's training was rough. I got a bout of pneumonia in late summer, at least I think that's what it was. I never went to the doctor, figuring it was probably viral anyway. That season I pulled double duty; we opened Energy Lab while I also kept my day job and managed IRONMAN training. On a related note, that's the year I taught myself to nap in a parked car.

I *tried* to stay in the crosswalk, but my preparation was a major fail. Training didn't happen how I'd pictured and wanted. Yet in my mind, missing Kona was not an option: tickets were booked, house on Ali'i was rented, and both John and my family were set to make the trip.

My amazing support crew: my parents and in-laws

So I toed the line anyway. I should have felt happy, but instead I felt trapped and worried that I wouldn't finish. Though the position I was in was my own fault, I felt like "not starting" was no option. My arms cramped on the swim since swimming to the coffee boat during race week—a long-time Kona tradition—was the most I'd swam in months. I also drank a lot of seawater which instigated an eight-hour stretch of vomiting. I barely paid attention to pacing on the bike, since just finishing would be a miracle. And on the run, there was more time spent walking than anything else. I did make it to the finish line that day, but it was a couple of hours past the time I'd planned.

Was the experience amazing? Yes, the experience as a whole was something I'll cherish forever. Should I have done something different, perhaps spectated the race or decided to tackle it another year instead? Who can say? By the grace of God, things turned out okay, and I didn't experience permanent illness or injury. But it could have easily gone the other way. On that day I learned a few valuable lessons that have carried over to life outside of tri.

Life is full of ambiguity—Have you missed so much training you're not sure whether you should tackle the race? Which obligations are okay to skip for the purposes of training? These questions can be tough to answer.

Learn from past mistakes—After Kona I vowed to never again tackle a race for which I was unprepared. Did I stick to that 100%? Heck no. But I did extricate myself out of a few sticky situations as a result of the lesson learned in Hawaii.

Commit to your decision—Once I decided to start the race, I was going to finish unless they dragged me off, or unless my excuse passed the DNF litmus test. What's the DNF litmus test? You can imagine yourself explaining to someone a week later why you absolutely had to quit.

It's okay to say no—My family and friends would have been disappointed if I'd bailed, but at the end of the day, we'd still have had a great time. Don't be afraid to say "no" or "not this time" if you're sure it's the best decision for you.

Part Three
Get Trained

You've clarified your why, you've gotten your gear, now it's finally time to start training.

In this section, we'll talk about how to prepare for training mentally and practically.

Then we'll talk a bit more about why you need training plan and how to read one.

Then we'll discuss each discipline separately: swim, bike, run, transition, and nutrition.

Finally, we'll cover putting everything together before race day.

13

TRAINING PEP TALK

You should follow a training plan instead of completely winging it. Why? Too much or too little training. And even if you stumble into the right formula, you'll lack confidence that you're properly prepared. Without a plan, you're prone to starting out strong and then petering out. This makes sense logically because if you don't know your destination how can you be expected to maintain motivation?

In the back of this book, we've included a plan to get you from couch to 5K as well as a beginner sprint tri plan. If you're looking for an intermediate or advanced plan, check out my website bethanyrutledge.com.

In the beginning, John and I didn't use a plan, and we were too intimidated to train with other athletes. We were particularly fearful of group bike rides. The solution? We just didn't go. Instead, we practiced on our own on the Silver Comet Trail. I figured shifting and clipping out on my own, albeit with plenty of spills along the way. But I also needed to ride safely with others and to navigate hills. So, with our first triathlon growing steadily closer, it was time to finally brave the group ride.

Our first ride with Atlanta Tri Club was a Saturday in March. It was still cold, and I wore the wrong clothes, pants that caught up in my chain. I didn't know how to shift, and it took some adjustment to adapt from my regular 30 rpms in a low gear. And I brought nothing to eat or drink; I didn't even have a bottle cage. I hadn't ridden long enough previously to require it. I remember feeling a sense of panic when we passed the Highway 278 bridge in Powder Springs, over 11 miles away from the start line, which marked the farthest I had ever ridden.

The rest of the story is that it turned out okay. Sure, I asked a few dumb questions, but no one cared. Instead, the fact that I was a newbie gave others permission to give advice. I soaked up helpful tips on shifting, nutrition, saddles, and more.

Being new isn't something to fear. Here are three reasons it pays to be a newb:

1. **People love to teach.** Whether it's asking for shifting advice or transition tips, triathletes love to help. They were all beginners once, too!

2. **You can ask for forgiveness versus permission.** This universally applicable phrase works well in triathlon. When you accidentally do something that goes against group norms, say, wearing an aero helmet during a training session or a full tri kit to a run race, you have a great built-in excuse.

3. **You're constantly celebrating achievements.** From tackling your first brick session to the finish line of your first race, being a newb means constantly celebrating small successes. It's a habit that will serve you well later where not every training session is a PR or new experience.

TOP BEGINNER DOS AND DON'TS

Ah! The anticipation before starting training is reminiscent of the first day of school. Worrying about how the heck you're going to make space to get everything done? Calculating how long it will take to dry your hair and get rid of goggle marks after a lunch swim? Here are a few general dos and don'ts as you plan your day one of training:

DO COMMIT TO JUST DOING IT.

After you've signed up for a race, told your friends, and tackled all the firsts of training, a lull in motivation can strike when you least expect. "Why am I doing this?" you may ask yourself.

Then you start skipping a training session here and there "because you don't feel like it." Before long, you'll reach a crossroads. Is this a goal worth tackling? And if so, how committed are you?

Dips in motivation are an inevitable part of the process. If you're not sick or injured, then the trick is to just do it anyway. One mental trick is committing to only part of the prescribed session. "I have a five-mile run today, but I might only do two." Chances are, once you reach two miles, you'll find new motivation to keep going.

Try to commit to just doing it 90% of the time whether you feel like or not. Once it becomes a habit and a part of your daily routine, there will be more days you *do* feel like exercising. And, even if you never get to the point of exercise addict, you will at least recognize you feel better afterwards.

DON'T GET SUCKED IN TO WINNING TRAINING.

Your first nonstop mile run, your first open water swim, your first bike ride with clip-ins. Beginner triathlon training is full of exciting milestones. This can go wrong when you start forcing it—putting pressure on yourself to PR and go faster and farther each ride or run. This is a good way to burn out, get injured, and ultimately stunt your progress. "Train slow to go fast" *is* a thing. That doesn't mean you'll never push yourself in training; it just means that not every training session should be a race.

DON'T GET CAUGHT UP IN THE FANCY STUFF.

It's easy to get overwhelmed with all the information and training data available. Should you eat sugar, go keto, run barefoot, or go vegan? What's the perfect interval protocol? I talk to athletes all the time who are overly focused on ground contact time or SWOLF score when they should be worried about getting to the pool three times a week and working up to consistent running! Commit to following your plan now and worry about Chrissie Wellington's favorite set later.

> **TERMS TO KNOW**
>
> **PR**—refers to "personal record," your best performance at that distance. Triathletes who want to improve their performance keep track of PRs. Example: "I had a great race and was only 20 seconds off my PR!" Closely related is CR, or course record, which refers to a best performance on a specific course. For example, your 5K PR may have been set on a flat course, yet you may set an equally or more impressive CR on a tough course.

BEGINNER TRAINING FAQS

How can I get over the intimidation of joining a group session? Is everyone going to be faster, younger, stronger, or cooler than me? The best way to get over intimidation is information. Call or email the person in charge. If it's a run group, you'll want to know if there are a variety of paces and distances within the group. For a swim, you'll want to know how many lanes are available and if swimmers are separated by ability level. And for cycling, you'll want to know whether the ride is "no drop" (meaning they won't leave someone behind) or not.

TIPS FOR A COMEBACK

Perhaps you were physically active in the past but took a break for a few weeks—or years. Whether you're struggling with extra pounds or a big gap in your old paces and endurance, here are a few quick tips for starting back.

Getting started again is the hardest part. While it may never be "fun" to wake up to a 5:30AM alarm, your first time back is the hardest. The longer you wait, the harder it will be. It can be tempting to keep putting off your "comeback" week after week. Remember that your future self will thank you for starting back now instead of in another week…or month!

Nothing's as hard as the first time. Assuming you've been in shape before, it's a faster process to come back physically than to start from the beginning. But it can be harder mentally since you're constantly comparing now and then. As hard as it is, let go of your old benchmarks and enjoy the positive reinforcement of new accomplishments.

Here are some tips for getting started again:

» **Don't start with something epic**—Starting out the first week with a 5K swim or a 3-hour group ride will only lead to feeling discouraged and overly sore.

» **Ditch the gadgets**—No need to wear your Garmin for those first few forays back into running. If you're competitive and metric driven, this can keep you from enjoying your run and building consistency.

» **Set a modest weekly goal**—For the first few weeks, go for the CDC recommended five hours of aerobic activity a week and two days of muscle strengthening activity.

» **Then, set an exciting future goal**—After a few weeks of exercising for health benefits, sign up for that destination race or a type of race you haven't tried before. It's important to have something exciting on the horizon.

14

TRAINING PLAN BASICS

In the beginning, I didn't follow a training plan, but I *had* them. In fact, I had several to compare to make sure I was doing enough. I printed them out; I logged my training on beginnertriathlete.com; I talked about them with my new tri buddies. This was before Strava, the ubiquitous social media training site, so there was more *talking* about training rather than *showing* data to back it up. (Which made others' exaggerated stories about their training exploits that much more intimidating!) The goal in this chapter is to cover the basics of your training plan and simplify things.

TOP BEGINNER DOS AND DON'TS

The term *training plan* sounds self-important and vaguely frightening. Some think of a training plan as having magical powers. Or maybe that was just me. Here are a few common dos and don'ts as you dive into to your training plan.

DO SET AN APPROPRIATE TIMELINE FOR TRAINING.

Life can foil or complicate your training timeline, and injury, illness, or extended travel can't always be predicted. With that in mind, take the following advice as a suggestion rather than as a mandate.

If you have no health barriers and have been cleared by your physician, you are ready to start. Where should you start? If you've been sedentary for the last six months, begin with a couch to 5K program before training for a triathlon. And if you're in decent physical condition, already exercising in the three sports, then consider training for an event 10 to 16 weeks out. Planning something six months from now that's achievable in a few weeks may not be an exciting enough carrot.

DON'T SKIP THE SKILL WORK.

An example is an athlete with no swim background who hits the pool daily to hammer out laps without working on her stroke first. It's swimming where this can be the most dangerous since it's the most technique-oriented sport. However, running and cycling with no attention to skill can also reinforce poor habits. You may still get faster initially because you're doing the sport more, but eventually poor form and lack of skill will become a limiter.

Instead, incorporate skill work into your training from the outset. Swimming is the most important sport to gain instruction. When my husband and I started training, this was one of the first and best tips we received. Though it was tempting to skip professional instruction, I have no doubt that it helped us in the long run. In fact, if I could go back, I would commit to more swim instruction before training the swim. Once you firm up that muscle memory, it's very hard to change habits later.

DON'T TRAIN TOO MUCH.

Since overtraining is a clinical syndrome and can be misleading, we'll call the issue "training more than appropriate" or "under-recovery." Many beginners (again, lacking a plan) want to train their favorite sport at the detriment of their area of opportunity. For example, if you're used to running daily, you may need to temporarily cut back to allow space for swim and bike. Using a plan will give you an idea of a balanced way to disperse your time and energy over the disciplines.

DO LOG YOUR TRAINING.

Whether it's marking off a printed plan or using an online training software like Strava or TrainingPeaks, commit to tracking your training. You need data to objectively assess your fitness. Perhaps you missed a week of training due to illness, and you're wondering whether you have enough fitness to take on your next race. Your past data gives you or your coach context to make these decisions.

It's too easy to misremember if you're not logging daily. How so? Our memories are fallible and typical memories of training are rife with hyperbole. "I used to run 20 miles a week," someone might say, then a peek at their training log reveals they ran 20 miles for *one* week back in 2010. Why does it matter? Because instead of someday wondering how you were possibly able to run so far or so much, you'll be able to fact check yourself for a more accurate picture.

Let's say your best running year ever was 2014. What were you doing then? What kind of mileage, volume, and intensity made you so fast? Having a history takes out the guesswork.

ELEMENTS OF A TRAINING PLAN

Now it's time to tackle the ins and outs of your training plan. I'm going to let you in on a little secret. When you're brand new, your number one priority is to build up the endurance to successfully get from the start line to the finish line safely. That's it. You don't *need* the fancy run intervals your fast friend told you about. You don't *have* to swim masters. You don't even actually *do* 100 percent of what's on the plan. Following a basic plan takes away the guesswork, the worry. Am I doing too much, too little, not enough? Is there anybody out there training the same as I am?

Let's talk about the principles that are at the heart of every training plan. At the most basic level, a training plan is a simple map to take you from where you are to where you want to be. And if you're using a training plan in this book, one you find online, or the one your friend recommended—unless it's written for you alone—it's a more general plan that may need some tweaking to fit you best.

PRINCIPLES OF TRAINING

In order to bring positive change, physical stress to the body is necessary, and its actually during recovery that we become stronger. This response is called adaption. Increasing the stress or stimulus to create further adaption is called progressive overload, and it is at the heart of every training plan. Stress can be increased or decreased by manipulating the three elements of training: workout frequency, workout duration, and workout intensity.

Frequency—How often you work out is the most basic element of training. For example, your training plan may have you swim two to three times/week, bike two to three times/week, and run two to four times/week.

Duration—Duration can be measured in terms of the distance covered or the elapsed time of the workout. Some workouts are long to build greater endurance, while others are short to allow more emphasis on higher intensities or to promote recovery. Your training plan will measure swim duration in yards, run duration by time, and cycling duration by time.

Intensity—Intensity is the measure of how hard you are working. Unlike frequency and duration, workout intensity is somewhat more difficult to quantify. The beginner training plan in this book uses RPE (rate of perceived exertion) to measure intensity.

SETTING HEART RATE ZONES WITH LACTATE THRESHOLD

Setting zones requires an anchor point. Without a reference point, "zone two" doesn't mean anything. Zone two of what? To populate heart rate zones, we first need to know your lactic threshold heart rate.

For heart rate to mean anything, you require a northern star, and that star is your lactic threshold heart rate. Lactate threshold (LT) refers to a point physiologically where lactate starts accumulating in the blood more quickly than it can be processed. The heart rate value that corresponds is called lactate threshold heart rate (LTHR).

If you look at any forum where new triathletes gather, there is still a lot of confusion over the use of heart rate and the proper use of zones. With the mainstream availability of wrist heart rate sensors in everything from Apple Watch to Garmin, more and more people have access to using heart rate, but sometimes that access lacks context. Thus, it is not unusual to hear athletes claiming to do all their runs in zone 5, perform three-hour rides at an IF of 1.2, or other impossible feats.

Instead of hitting an exercise physiology lab, most amateur athletes use field tests to find this value. During the test you will perform an all-out, 30-minute effort. The average heart rate of the last 20 minutes of that effort is your LTHR. Your running LT and cycling LT are not the same and should be tested separately. In the intermediate and advanced plans available at BethanyRutledlge.com, we use Joe Friel's HR training zones (see the *Triathlete Training Bible* by Joe Friel), which are based on your lactate threshold heart rate (LTHR). If you use heart rate in training or intend to, testing is of the utmost importance; 220 minus age is *not* a reliable way to set zones, nor are the default settings in Garmin Connect. Using those values will only serve to confuse and frustrate you.

As an intermediate or experienced athlete, one of the first things you will do in the training plan is test in all three sports. In some cases, it may not be appropriate to test right away in all three sports, for example, if you just started running or have an injury. After testing, your workouts will be communicated in zones.

Simple Run and Bike LTHR Test:

» Perform an easy 10-minute warm-up.

» Perform a 30-minute time trial, capturing your heart rate average for the last 20 minutes.

» Input that value into TrainingPeaks or other online calculator or use the following chart to find your values.

Your running and cycling heart rate thresholds will be different values, so be sure to do both tests!

HEART RATE ZONES

Running Zones

Zone 1	Less than 85% of LTHR
Zone 2	85 to 89% of LTHR
Zone 3	90 to 94% of LTHR
Zone 4	95 to 99% of LTHR
Zone 5a	100 to 102% of LTHR
Zone 5b	103 to 106% of LTHR
Zone 5c	More than 106% of LTHR

Cycling Zones

Zone 1	Less than 81% of LTHR
Zone 2	81 to 89% of LTHR
Zone 3	90 to 93% of LTHR
Zone 4	94 to 99% of LTHR
Zone 5a	100 to 102% of LTHR
Zone 5b	103 to 106% LTHR
Zone 5c	More than 106% of LTHR

PERIODIZATION

Periodization simply means dividing training into chunks and focusing each period on different aspects of fitness. Each section will look different in terms of frequency, intensity, and volume of the three sports. As your goal race approaches, your training will move from general (less like the race) to specific (more like the race).

For our purposes, periodization needn't be complicated. For absolute beginner athletes, the most important factor is developing the endurance to get to the finish line while building volume safely with appropriate recovery periods.

DEALING WITH SETBACKS

The goal? Checking off each day's session with no barriers, interruptions, or setbacks. The reality? Things often don't go as planned. Don't become discouraged when inevitable setbacks occur. The following things happen to everyone:

» Something hurts.

» Work, family, or life gets in the way.

» You or a family member gets sick.

» You temporarily lose motivation.

It's what you do next that determines your ultimate success. After a setback, rekindle your motivation by remembering what inspired you in the first place.

What happens if I miss a few days?

» If you miss a couple of days to one week of training, then take a few easy ramp-up days and continue into the current week on the plan.

» If you miss more than five days of training, you may need a longer period of reduced training/ramp-up to get back on track.

» Whatever you do, do not try to make up all the missed sessions. You can rearrange future sessions if you miss a few priority workouts (long workouts), but don't try to cram everything in or you could injure yourself!

What if I am too tired to complete a session? There will inevitably be days where you have trouble completing a session as prescribed. This is completely normal. You have a couple of choices when this happens: You can shuffle around workouts, skip it, or try to revisit the workout later.

Your key sessions in the beginner plan are your long swims, rides, and runs. If you miss a *key* session, do your best to fit it in when you are well rested and have the time to tackle that session, even if it means dropping or rearranging something else.

BEGINNER PLAN AT A GLANCE

METRICS

Bike—For the purposes of this book, our plan will use RPE (rate of perceived exertion). The intermediate and advanced website plans (available at bethanyrutledge.com) will also use heart rate and power zones.

Run—Again, our plan will use RPE and the advanced plans will use heart rate and pace.

Swim—This plan uses RPE. The advanced plans use pace (i.e., 2:00/100 yards or meters).

Recovery workouts—Zones and paces are not used for recovery sessions. Particularly in the case of runs, we want these days to be truly easy and not focus on maintaining a set pace. Keep the easy days easy, so on the hard days you can truly go hard!

Rate of perceived exertion is a way to subjectively describe effort levels. In your training plan we'll use the following scale.

RPE SCALE (RATE OF PERCEIVED EXERTION)

1	Very light—an effort level you could continue "forever" if someone kept feeding you. A "walk to the mailbox" level. This zone is used for recovery, warm-up, and cool-down.
2	Fairly light—You feel like you're doing something, but you can easily carry on long conversations or concentrate on an audiobook. This corresponds to your everyday bread-and-butter runs or endurance workouts.
3	Moderate—You can speak in short sentences, though you may have to concentrate to keep up this effort level for more than an hour.
4	Somewhat hard—The effort level you can sustain for about an hour during a race, less during training. Roughly corresponds to your Z4, around your LTHR.
5	Hard—Can only sustain for a few minutes at a time before you'll have to slow or stop. These efforts should be avoided in a race (save for your finish line sprint).

TERMS YOU MAY SEE

Not all these terms will be in your beginner training plan, but here's some verbiage you'll see along your training journey.

SWIMMING TERMINOLOGY

Swim (S)	Swim
Drill (D)	Insert choice drill or listed drill
Kick (K)	Kicking only, with or without board
Pull (P)	Pull with a pull buoy
Stroke (Stk)	Something other than freestyle
Sprint (Sp)	All-out effort
Warm-up (WU)	Easy mix of swim strokes and drills prior to the main set
Cool-down (CD)	Last set, used to relax and warm down
Descend	Easy set gets gradually faster or harder in effort
Notation of (x") to the right	Indicates rest between intervals for instance 10 x 100 (10") means with 10 seconds rest between each
On	Instead of indicating rest periods, sometimes you will be assigned a time to leave on. For example, 10 x 100 on 2' means you leave for each successive 100 on the two-minute mark.

CYCLING TERMINOLOGY

Climb	A cadence range between approximately 55-70 RPMs
Flat or race cadence	A cadence range between approximately 80-90 RPMs
Sprint (or high cadence)	Refers to a cadence above 95 RPMs
Isolated leg training (ILT)	Isolated leg training—unclip one foot and maintain a smooth pedal stroke with the remaining leg while cycling at a low power, usually 50-60% FTP
Spin-up	During the time interval specified, start with a moderate cadence and gradually build to as fast as you can spin while still maintaining a smooth pedal stroke.
Functional threshold power	Defined as the maximum power you can sustain for a period of one hour. We base your training zones off of this metric

RUNNING TERMINOLOGY

400, 800, 1600	Refers to laps around a standard distance track
5K, 10K, HMP, or MP	Refers to the pace of your last 5K, 10K, half marathon, or marathon
Fartlek	Swedish for "speed play;" variable pace running without specific times assigned to intervals
Intervals	Training in which short, fast amounts of running are alternated with slower periods of recovery running. For example, "six times 400 meters fast [these are the repeats] with 400-meter recovery jogs [the intervals]."
Strides	Short, fast, but controlled runs of 50-150 meters. Strides, which are used both in training and to warm up before a race, build speed and efficiency.
Tempo runs	Sustained effort training runs at zone 3 pace
Threshold runs	Threshold pace is roughly equivalent to what exercise physiologists call "lactate threshold," or the point at which your muscles start fatiguing at a rapid rate. Zone 4 pace.

TRAINING BASICS FAQS

How can I run easy when all running feels hard? This is an issue that will get better with consistency and time. It may be appropriate for you to start with run–walk intervals.

Do I have to use heart rate? Going by RPE, the rate of perceived exertion, is perfectly fine. Check the tables to get an idea of the scale of perceived exertion.

Can I take more days off? Your plan is designed with one day off per week. Feel free to shuffle sessions and take additional days as needed. In an ideal world, you'll get in 90% of the plan. That said, if you complete 75% of the plan—and don't neglect the swim— you should be able to complete the race.

What if I was a college swimmer (or runner or cyclist)? This plan is general. You may need to tweak it to meet your needs. For example, if you're training for a marathon, you will want to run more, and if you were a college swimmer, you may want to replace some swim sessions with your weakest sport.

#TriLessons: Tackling Your Training Plan

In 2010, after I hired a coach and started using TrainingPeaks, I found a whole new level of training plan obsession. TrainingPeaks is an interactive software where your coach assigns your daily workouts in a calendar. After completing the session, you upload your file, allowing the coach to provide input, analyze, then assign the next training. It also has a very simple feature that has driven many an athlete mad: If you don't complete the assigned session or go over or under the planned time by more than 50%, that calendar day will show up red. If you only completed 50 to 79% of workout or went over by 121 to 150%, the day will show up yellow.

Of course, now that I have a perspective from the other side of the computer screen, I advise other athletes not to live or die by whether your TrainingPeaks week is green—denoting a week where all sessions went as planned. Here are other things I wish someone had told me about training plans—what to worry about and what to not stress about.

Don't Worry About These Things
How fast you go on your easy day—Forget pace and speed on an easy run or ride day. The point of a slow day is to promote recovery and blood flow. Trying to keep to your personal definition of a "good" power or pace during a recovery day will come back to haunt you in the form of poor recovery for key sessions. Instead, use recovery days to run with a slower friend, catch up on a podcast, or relax your mind without worrying about metrics.

Not getting it perfect—There will inevitably be days when a session is a miss or even a fail. Doing everything perfectly is not a good goal. Look at it this way: If you always hit everything perfectly, it's likely your training is too easy.

Tweaking training to fit life—Did you run out of time for your whole swim set on Tuesday and abbreviate the warm-up? Did you need to change an easy bike and run day into a brick due to time constraints? Small changes like this are not a big deal and are the reality of a busy life.

A bad workout—One bad session does not require a drastic overhaul to the plan. A succession of misses does. There is a good deal of gray area as to when to shorten, cut intensity, or bail completely on a key session. In general, for beginner triathletes, the duration is the most important thing. So if you're not sick, injured, or on the verge, keep duration even if it means you have to lower intensity that day. For example, let's say your assignment was to ride for two hours with 2 x 20' intervals in Zone 3. You start your first interval and realize quickly that it's just not going to happen. Your first tweak to the workout would be to still ride two hours (the assigned duration) and drop the intervals.

Do Worry About These Things
No workouts completed as planned—As mentioned, duration is key. So if you're constantly changing or cutting workouts short, you aren't following your plan.

Bailing on a specific type of session—Often the training we dislike is the training we need most. If you're a track star who loves 200s and 400s yet hates running more than a mile, guess what? There's a good chance that endurance at a lower intensity are the things you most need to work on.

Never having fun—This one may sound strange, but in my experience, athletes who don't enjoy training and the sport don't tend to stick around long. Sure it's not always fun to pop out of bed at 4AM to jump into a cold pool, but you should be getting rewarded on some level aside from race day.

15

SWIM TRAINING

At the onset of my training, swim training seemed daunting. Do people really wear those ugly, high-necked bathing suits? Why do I get gassed and have to stop at the wall to hyperventilate after each lap? And how can you effectively "train" if you're taking constant breaks? We'll tackle these questions and more during this section.

TOP BEGINNER DOS AND DON'TS

If you've read the other sections, you've come to the swim armed with goggles, a suit, and a swim cap. Now it's time to train! Here are the top five dos and don'ts for beginning swim training.

Swimming with friends is always more fun.

DO GET EXPERT HELP.

Unless you swam in high school or college, get expert eyes on your stroke before you start training. In a perfect world, that would include a one-on-one lesson. If it includes video analysis, that's even better. If that's simply not possible, then have a coach at a masters group or an experienced friend check out your stroke and offer suggestions as a good starting point. Some coaches offer a virtual service where you send a video and then receive personalized drills and feedback. Learn more about this Energy Lab service here: energylabatl.com.

DON'T SWIM AS MUCH AS POSSIBLE.

Invest in the previous steps before getting into a regular schedule of "workouts." If you're excited, it will be hard to do this. This doesn't mean you shouldn't swim in the meantime, though. You should practice your drills and gradually increase your swim volume at the rate recommended by your swim instructor. How much and how soon will vary widely depending on the stroke you start with and how it develops. Try to practice the drills for just a few minutes before every swim workout or practice. Frequency is the key here, not volume.

DO JOIN A SWIM GROUP.

If you swam in early life, you can probably jump right into a masters or triathlon specific swim group and get back up to speed just fine. If not, you'll want to do some research on beginner swim groups, or ask if they have a beginner lane available. For instance at our tri club swim practices, we have a dedicated beginner lane with a dedicated coach. These swimmers enjoy individualized attention so they can develop good stroke habits from the outset.

DO LEARN BILATERAL BREATHING.

Although it's tempting to breathe only on your favored side, learn or practice bilateral breathing from the start. There will be times you don't use it, but practicing bilateral during the warm-up and cool-down will help develop a symmetrical stroke.

DO SWIM FREQUENTLY.

Swimming responds best to frequency when you're developing your technique. So it's better to devote four sessions of 30 minutes per week then two two-hour sessions.

SWIMMING HURDLES TO TACKLE

Here are a few of the most common beginner swim issues. If you're new to swimming, no doubt one or more will describe you.

GETTING GASSED QUICKLY

Athletes are often surprised at how tough it is to add distance during those first swims, even if they're regularly participating in another aerobic sport. If you run miles with ease yet get completely gassed after 25 or 50 yards in the pool, don't worry. This phenomenon is completely normal and occurs because the swim is so technique oriented. Thus, the world record holder in the 10K could jump in the pool and have the exact same issue. It doesn't matter how "fit" you are, you need some technique!

The Fix: Get help with your stroke so you can ingrain good habits! Be patient and commit to practicing several times a week.

ADDING DISTANCE

When you're only able to swim 25 or 50 yards without a break, stringing together 400 yards seems impossible! At this stage, swimming at all is such a high-intensity, taxing effort that adding on distance isn't possible. But once you can "swim easy" enough to make 400, it's no big deal to continue to add.

The Fix: You must learn how to swim easy and what's preventing you from doing so. You have to master the stroke mechanics to make swimming sustainable. Again, this comes back to the expert eye on your stroke. Maybe your problem is rotation, body position, or kicking too hard. Continued stroke technique and training will teach you to swim "easy," which will help you swim longer.

INSERT YOUR OWN EXCUSE

It's all too easy to say things like "I'm too muscular, I sink right to the bottom" when in fact there are plenty of people shorter, more muscular, or leaner who swim just fine. We all have an excuse. My personal favorite is that I thought swim team was lame in high school. And before that—at summer camp—I avoided swimming because of ear infections. Now, of course, I would like to go back in time and learn good stroke habits at a young age.

The Fix: Realize we all come from different backgrounds and have different strengths and weaknesses. We're all doing the best we can with what we have!

THE IMPORTANCE OF OPEN WATER SWIMMING

As I stood in a cold lake preparing to tackle the John Tanner Sprint, I desperately wished I had done more open water swimming.

A swim buddy is a must.

When the horn went off, the water became a churning mess of arms and legs. I got whacked and kicked more times than I could count, which increased my panic. I stopped and apologized to about the first three people I made contact with. "Oh, I'm sorry." "Whoops!" After that, I realized no one was apologizing to me, and when I grazed these ladies with my hand or foot, they didn't even break stroke!

In the middle of that lake, I finally appreciated the value of open water swim practice and swimming with a group regularly. The only way to get used to swimmer contact is to swim with others, and the only way to properly practice swimming open water is to just do it. Yes, it's time consuming. Yes, it's hard to find a place, and the water is likely cold. But open water swimming is still one of the most important training sessions you can do to set yourself up for success.

You'll never hear a first-time triathlete say that they wish they had spent *less* time in open water prior to the race. They always wish they had practiced more!

FINDING OPEN WATER SWIMS

Don't swim alone. You may not know anyone (yet) who swims in local lakes for fun, but they're out there. Here we'll discuss finding swim company.

» **Triathlon groups**—Many tri groups have organized or informal outings. Depending on how official the swim is (do they have kayaks? Coaches?), there may be a nominal fee, or swimmers may throw in a few bucks to help pay a lifeguard.

» **Coached open water swims**—There's nothing like hands-on help with skills, such as entry, exit, rounding a buoy, drafting, and sighting (most important).

» **Special events or clinics**—Search online or use active.com to find clinics that cover the basics of open water swimming. For instance, a race director here hosts several free open water clinics on a sprint race course.

Again, don't swim alone! For swim safety, purchase a swim buoy such as the New Wave Swim Buoy (newwaveswimbuoy.com). This device, though not an official life-saving device, will make you more visible to boats and is something to grab on to while you're floating.

BEGINNERSWIMMERBESTPRACTICESSUMMARY

» **Try private lessons.** Use the internet or ask for a personal recommendation from a friend.

» **Swim with a group.** Try swimming with a masters group or triathlete-specific swim program.

» **Mix it up.** Don't be afraid to try different things such as learning to swim different strokes, playing with pool toys, or, gasp, learning to flip turn. Remember that half the battle is keeping it fun!

» **Practice to improve.** One to two times a week will only help you maintain. Swim three times a week or more to get better.

» **Incorporate bilateral breathing and drill work during the warm-up portion.**

» **Practice open water as much as possible, especially at the beginning of your swim journey.**

QUICK STEPS TO START SWIMMING

» Purchase swimsuit, goggles, and swim cap.

» Start out with group or individual swim lessons.

» Practice three times per week to improve your stroke.

» Start doing swim "workouts" after stroke work.

» Continue to practice assigned drills during the warm-up of each workout.

» After you can comfortably swim two times the distance of your race (for a sprint), look for open water swim opportunities.

» Practice in open water as many times as possible before your race.

BEGINNER SWIMMING FAQS

How do I count distances in an Olympic pool? One *length* is 25 yards and is often called a 25. A *50* is down to the end of the pool and back. A *100* is four lengths, and so forth. A *lap* typically means a 50, or down to the end and back.

How do I read a swim workout? Typically, a swim workout has a warm-up, drill set, main set, and cool-down. A very simple swim workout may read something like this:

» 200 warm-up. (Typically, freestyle or a mix of strokes if you know how to do other strokes.)

» 4 x 50 drill. (Work on a specific part of your stroke.)

» 10 x 100 (20"). (10 x 100 yards at a moderate effort level with 20 seconds of rest in between each.)

» 200 cool-down. (Typically freestyle or a mix of strokes.)

Do I need to know other strokes? Learning strokes other than freestyle has value. If you attend a swim practice comprised of mostly triathletes, you won't see a lot of other stroke work included in your set (such as the dreaded butterfly). However, it's worth taking the time to learn at least a rudimentary backstroke and breaststroke. Backstroke is a great stroke to know so you can flip over on your back to rest during a race. Breaststroke is great to know in case you're having trouble sighting during a race.

What is sighting? Sighting is the practice of lifting your head to sight buoys or landmarks during an open water swim or race. When performed correctly, it is initiated when you reach with your breathing side arm before the pull phase of the stroke. Done well, it should not break the rhythm of your stroke. Typical frequency of sighting varies, but once every five strokes is a good starting point.

Can I wear a normal bathing suit? One important investment is a new swimsuit. A typical, sunbathing-at-the-beach swimsuit will gap and cause drag, which you don't want, especially as a beginner. You also have a much greater chance of a "wardrobe malfunction."

Are swim lessons really worth it? Swim lessons, like any one-to-one service, are expensive. Yet they're also a worthwhile investment. The stroke you develop now, with habits good and bad, will be much, much harder to change once your muscle memory is set.

BEYOND BEGINNER SWIMMING

Should you do a swim focus to improve? What about spending the winter months on swimming? Whether to swim way more—or as little as possible—remains a popular debate among triathletes. Just to summarize the common arguments on both sides, here they are:

Reasons NOT to swim

» The swim is only a small percentage of the race overall, so potential time savings is small.

» More potential gains possible from the other sports. For example, you might have a couple potential minutes of time gain on the swim, but dozens of minutes to gain by improving your bike or run.

» For various reasons, potentially saving 5 to 10 minutes total isn't worth putting in a ton of extra training time.

» You are not a skilled swimmer, but you're skilled enough to finish, and that's your primary goal.

Reasons IN FAVOR of swimming (more)

» You're an injury-prone athlete who wants to improve your overall aerobic fitness.

» You care about improvement in all areas and have time to devote to all three sports.

» Your swim time is not up to par, limiting you in some way (i.e., close to cutoff time or the thing keeping you out of awards).

» You didn't grow up swimming and are an unskilled swimmer who could make a lot of gains through simple technique changes.

Let's say that you've decided on a swim focus. The next step is deciding your best path to improvement. Everyone can benefit from improving their technique, so that's a great place to start. Yet technique can only take you so far, so at some point, more swimming and harder swimming have to come into play.

To improve your swim fitness, start by increasing the frequency of swim practices. Be sure to incorporate harder intervals. For fitness gains, you must do more than swim slowly up and down the pool. Next, incorporate intervals, starting with shorter ones that allow you to maintain good form. You can start out with intervals as short as 25s and 50s. Over the course of the season you will then progress to longer intervals.

#TriLessons: Megan's Top Fixes for Common Swim Issues

Megan Melgaard, longtime swim coach and former Olympic Trials qualifier, has helped hundreds of triathletes in her 22 years of coaching. She shares a few common problems she sees with "adult onset swimmers."

Breathing—Breathing issues are a common culprit for new triathletes who have trouble adding distance or swimming with "ease." Breathing out too forcefully or holding your breath can tire you out quickly. "Try and relax the breath by sighing out the air or softly humming. You shouldn't sound like a motorboat on the exhale or gasp for the inhale," Megan advises. "The strength of your exhalations should correspond to how hard you're swimming." Timing of the exhalations is also important. You should exhale underwater, not after the mouth has breached the surface of the water.

Breathing position—A common issue is pressing the arm, opposite from the breathing side, down while the head is turned in the breathing position. Instead, the arm should stay extended while in the breathing position to create lift and stability, almost like an airplane wing, rather than pressing down, becoming off balance and creating drag. In addition, favoring one side while breathing can lead to asymmetric rotation. "If you only breathe to one side, keep conscious of symmetric rotation on the non-breathing side."

Practice—Catch-up drill and catch-up drill with a kickboard to train the arm to stay out in the extended position while breathing. One-arm drills, with or without a kickboard, may also help with focus on the breathing movement.

Poor body position—Another common limiter is body position. Frequent issues are sinking legs, swimming uphill, and swinging hips from side to side. There are a few cues you can visualize to improve your body position. First, focus on activating the core by standing tall—like when you are getting measured for height at the doctor's office. Second, utilize proper head position by focusing the gaze toward the bottom of the pool versus looking forward. Third, monitor leg position in relation to the surface. Your heels should breach the surface of the water when kicking. Additionally, ensure during rotation that your shoulder and hip rotate in line versus rotating only from the shoulder, which often causes the hips to swing from side to side.

Practice—Pull with a buoy in between the ankles to feel proper body position. Keep legs from swinging side to side by swimming tall, which will help engage core to keep muscles activated and body streamlined. Consider adding a snorkel to maintain proper head position. Side kicks and hesitation drills like "six kick switch" will help focus on body position and in-line rotation.

Kicking problems—The third issue Megan commonly sees is with kicking. "It is typical to see new swimmers kick from their knees. Kicking should come from your hip flexor area." Begin the kick by moving the upper leg from the hip area and allowing the knee to bend very slightly. Keep the ankles relaxed and toes pointed back. The proper position of the foot then generates water moving backwards, which then propels the swimmer. Kicking not only helps with propulsion, but also balances and aids in rotation. Be cautious of over-pointing the toes, which can lead to calf cramps.

Practice—Sit on a step or the side of the pool and kick by slightly moving the hip joint and slightly bending the knee to generate power from the upper leg into extension. Try and kick the water away from you. Then, kick with both hands on the wall with the body straight, head in line. Flutter the feet.

16

CYCLING TRAINING

My first bike ride as an adult was memorable. In a rush to start training, I went to the first place I thought of that sold bikes, Play It Again Sports. It seemed like a great idea; I could get a bargain and a bike immediately. They had exactly one road bike, and it was $400, much less than the price of a new bike at the store. It seemed a little…large…but I figured I would make it work.

I invited a friend to ride on a local rails-to-trails path. I jumped on and started pedaling in my run shorts and running shoes atop clipless pedals. Slowly—because I didn't know how to switch gears and I could barely even reach the handlebars! We went for an eight-mile ride, or maybe it was six, and it was an absolutely torturous experience.

My bike didn't fit, I couldn't shift gears, clip in, or endure the pain of riding more than a few miles at a time. How was I ever going to even finish the bike leg of a sprint tri much less become a strong, competent rider? Because of reading this book, you're already several steps ahead of where I was!

Powering to T2 at IRONMAN Chattanooga 70.3 2017

TOP BEGINNER DOS AND DON'TS

If you've read the section on what you need, then you you're armed with a bike that you bought, borrowed, or stole, a kit or some shorts, a helmet, a way to carry hydration and nutrition, a flat kit, and the knowledge of how to use it. Now let's get to training! Here are some top dos and don'ts for getting started.

DO KEEP THINGS SIMPLE.

You have plenty of time to worry about metrics, power, interval schemes, and progression later. For your first race, what's important is your endurance—building up to the distance you will ride and riding frequently enough to build fitness. Aside from that, your number one priority is safety, which means learning the rules of the road, clipping in and out, and riding with traffic and other cyclists.

DON'T LET LACK OF BIKE ACCESS DETER YOU.

Many beginners join our tri club without a bike. We encourage these athletes to train in a spin class or cycling studio. Eventually, you'll want to ride outside on the bike you'll use on race day, but don't let lack of a bike deter you from getting started!

DO LEARN BASIC RIDING SKILLS.

If available, a group cycling lesson or beginner cyclists ride is a great place to start. For instance, we host a beginner cyclist clinic a few times a year where we review basics such as shifting gears, clipping in and out, safety, and more.

DO RIDE WITH OTHERS.

Riding with a group is also great for safety reasons. Even if you don't feel comfortable riding in traffic or on the main roads, you should know the etiquette of doing so. After all, during a race, you'll be riding with others on at least partly open roads. Check with a bike shop or local tri club to find out more about group rides. A lot of shops also have women-specific rides, which although not necessary can limit the intimidation factor somewhat.

DO RIDE OUTSIDE.

If you have a bike trainer or indoor option, you can do a large portion of your bike training inside. However, you need to do some training outside. A good way to split it up is by doing your longer ride outdoors and your two shorter sessions indoors each week. Handling skills, confidence with other riders, clipping in and out, and fitness to ride over varied terrain are a few of the skills best practiced outdoors.

CYCLING HURDLES TO TACKLE

The journey to becoming a confident, competent rider starts with work on these issues:

HANDLING SKILLS

Put simply, handling skills include all of the following:

»   How to pick up bottles and food while riding. How to navigate around obstacles and traffic safely.

»   How to clip in and out quickly and efficiently while the bike is moving.

»   How to hold your line and maintain proper distance while riding with others.

You'll develop many of these skills naturally as you ride more. One best practice is to ride frequently with more experienced cyclists and seek to emulate them. A parking lot (without cars) or a grassy field, is a great place to practice skills.

If you have trouble taking one hand off the handlebar to pick up a bottle or nutrition, then start by picking up your hand for short periods of time. For instance, take off your right hand and count to 10. Then try the same with your left hand. Repeat that three times during your ride. Each time you ride increase the time until your comfortable holding on with one hand.

Use the same principle to practice clipping in and out. If you have a trainer at home, you can practice becoming comfortable clipping out with your right leg, then your left leg. It's normal to favor one leg, but learn to clip out with both. After you've gotten comfortable, then it's time to move outside. If you can practice in a parking lot or the field first, do it. It's normal to have a few spills while mastering this skill.

Drafting, or riding too closely in another rider's slipstream, is illegal in triathlon because it confers an unfair advantage. USA Triathlon mandates three bike lengths between riders. Do most of your rides without drafting, both to practice for race day and for safety reasons. It's very unsafe to ride closely behind another rider with a tri bike because (unless you have electronic shifting) your hands aren't on the brakes.

THE ROLE OF CADENCE

You may already be familiar with the terms RPM (revolutions per minute) or cadence. For brand new riders, pedaling at a cadence over 80 can seem unnatural at first. The goal is to find a gear in which you can pedal smoothly, avoiding both the choppiness of dead spots with a too easy gear and hammering too big of a gear. If you have a sensor that allows you to monitor cadence, then practice a cadence between 80 to 90 during workouts. This will necessitate using all your gears.

Cadence is important, but focusing on RPMs alone won't get you anywhere. If you've been to a gym spin class, you've seen people bouncing all over the saddle at extremely high RPMs with little to no resistance. They may be burning calories, but they're not improving their real ride performance. The power you produce and ultimately the speed at which you ride is determined by combining two things: the force you're putting on the pedals and the speed at which the pedals are turning.

A typical triathlon mantra is "spin to win," but is high cadence really the best solution for everyone? Long-time advocates of high-cadence cycling will point to the classic example of Lance versus Jan Ulrich. Lance rode away from Jan with his higher cadence compared to Jan's preferred lower cadence style. The truth is, Lance was just a better cyclist overall, one who happened to prefer a higher cadence riding style. The same is true for you. Your best cycling performance may be achieved on a range of normal cadence as opposed to always pushing for higher cadences.

But doesn't cycling at a high cadence save your legs for the run? Higher cadence advocates point to studies showing that study participants performed better on a subsequent post-cycle run than subjects who cycled at a slow cadence. There are conflicting studies that show better running success at various cadences. What matters is that you train to run well after cycling at race pace intensity by practicing adequately during training efforts.

How does power work with cadence? Power (watts) is simply torque (force put on the pedal) times rotational speed (cadence). Low cadence = high force = more fast-twitch muscle recruitment whereas a higher cadence = lower force = more slow-twitch fiber recruitment. A higher cadence makes the work performed more tolerable to the muscle. It recruits less high-twitch fibers and "burns fewer matches." Cycling at a higher cadence also tends to stress your cardiovascular system more.

Conversely, cycling at a lower cadence stresses your muscular system. It also recruits more muscle fibers overall as well as more fast-twitch fibers. As far as your cardiovascular system goes, lower cadence cycling costs less in terms of oxygen consumption. In fact, studies have shown that cycling at an ultra-low cadence (40-60 RPMs) uses the least percentage of VO_2max for a given effort.

Cadence selection overall is not an either/or proposition. Your personal strengths, weaknesses, and physiological makeup determines your optimal cadence. Someone who is training regularly at a variety of cadences will eventually find their optimal cadence for training and racing. But you should also train your non-preferred way to increase your comfort level at various cadences and to improve your fitness. Over-gearing, or training at slower cadences, can help you develop strength whereas practicing pedaling with a higher cadence, at a range of intensities, can help improve pedaling efficiency. For beginners, form work such as one-leg pedaling drills and spin-ups can also help your pedal stroke.

Don't let a preoccupation with cadence cloud what's really important, making sure you develop the ability to maintain your goal power through your most efficient application of cadence during your goal event.

TRAINING INDOORS

Performing some of your training indoors is time efficient. Maybe you've considered using an indoor bike trainer, but the number of choices seems daunting. If you plan to cycle indoors, here is what you need to get started. (Note: If you have any specific questions about equipment, talk to the good folks at your local bike shop.)

TRAINER RIDING NECESSITIES

1. **The bike**—Any bike will do, but if you use a mountain bike, you should replace the rear tire with a smooth one.

2. **The trainer**—dcrainmaker.com is a great starting place for reviews of all levels of trainer.

3. **A way to collect data**—This can be as simple as a stopwatch or a clock on the wall. If you're using heart rate, you'll need a heart rate monitor. If you want to purchase a head unit that can connect with a possible future power meter, you need to consider that, too. Check out the product reviews on dcrainmaker.com for great articles that evaluate many of the popular head unit/watch options.

TRAINER RIDING EXTRAS AND TIPS

1. **Use a fan**—Contrary to what some believe, going without a fan is not a sign of being hardcore, it's actually limiting you.

2. **Set up a dedicated area**—When the 5AM alarm goes off, you'll be much more likely to get up and go if your "pain cave" is set up and ready. Even finding appropriate attire or putting your bike on your trainer can sound tough early in the morning.

3. **Get some guidance**—This can be anything from scripted workouts from your coach to an online plan to a Trainer Road plan (trainerroad.com).

4. **Pick your motivation**—Notice I used the word *motivation* versus *entertainment*. In my mind, entertainment, like watching a movie or reading a book (how do people do that!), mostly precludes working hard. To each his own, but I think pure music, or if you're especially masochistic, staring at a white wall while thinking about your next race, is a better motivator.

5. **Focus efforts with metrics**—Even as a newbie, you need an objective way to garner data and measure progress. Training with metrics—like power or heart rate—allows you to set your baseline, set up appropriate workouts, and ultimately measure the results of those workouts.

#TriLessons: Mastering Indoor Riding

Michelle Crossman had an old rickety trainer at home that she hardly used. But once she discovered riding with others indoors in a group setting, she was hooked. "After I discovered how hard you could actually push yourself indoors and rapidly improve with metrics, intervals, and focused workouts, I liked it so much I decided to up my home game by getting a KICKR and Zwift."

Just a few years later, Michelle is an indoor cycling instructor, USA Triathlon certified triathlon coach, and staunch advocate of indoor riding for all levels. She even rode 400 miles indoors last January as part of a contest—for fun!

I didn't love indoor riding at first either. As a new triathlete I had a basic trainer and no idea what kind of workouts to do. I had no power meter, no heart rate, and no plan. Consequently, I spent too many afternoons dodging cars in Atlanta traffic. Where I live, in-town riding is risky at best, and totally reckless at worst, so something had to change.

My view of indoor training started to shift in 2010 when I began two structured indoor sessions per week under my coach at the time, Meredith Kessler. I invested in a power meter to help quantify my intervals, and it was a whole new world. Rather than wondering whether I was going too hard, too easy, or thinking "is this even doing anything," I had a plan with objective metrics to hit.

My husband, John, and our friend, Ted, loved the idea of a place where our friends could complete these sessions together. Along with Atlanta Tri Club founder, Jim Boylan, we opened Energy

Lab, a power-based indoor cycling studio next to our bike shop partner, Podium Multisport.

Since we started our studio in 2012, indoor cycling has become more popular, and many athletes have advanced power-based trainers in their own basements.

Making Indoors Fun
Spinning easy while watching a movie, although okay for recovery or an absolute beginner, won't get you very far. If your goal is to improve, you need metrics to make that workout count. If you don't have a coach or training plan, consider starting with Sufferfest, TrainerRoad, or Zwift to "outsource" the specifics of training.

Don't know what I'm talking about? There are many current options to game-ify your training. Here's a few of the best and most popular:

1. **Zwift**—If you're into video games (or even if you're not), Zwift is an amazing multiplayer, interactive platform where you can ride with cyclists all over the world using your bike as an online avatar. You can use any trainer, but adding in a heart rate monitor, speed and cadence sensor, or power meter, you can accurately ride in group rides, taking advantage of drafting and even climb mountains.

2. **Sufferfest**—These tough and humorous training videos have come a long way. Don't be turned off by the name, the powers-that-be at Sufferfest definitely have a sense of humor that shines through in their tough but entertaining workout videos. You can pair your sensors with an app like Zwift, but you can also just follow along and do the intervals by feel.

3. **TrainerRoad**—TR has a vast menu of workouts and plans that you can also link up with your sensors (or not). You can filter their library of workouts by purpose, length, or any number of other criteria.

BEGINNER CYCLING BEST PRACTICES

» Find something to ride and practice on it before your first tri. Make sure it's safe for riding by taking it to a bike shop.

» Practice the basics—stopping, starting, shifting gears, and safely riding with others.

» Make sure it's no big deal to ride the distance of your race before race day.

» After your first race(s), research and make an informed decision on a bike purchase.

» Make the first step of your shopping obtaining a proper bike fit.

QUICK STEPS TO START CYCLING

» Beg, borrow, or steal a bike (*not* your dream bike yet).

» Become comfortable shifting, mounting, dismounting, riding with others, and clipless pedals if using them.

» Ride three times a week if possible with one of those rides being outdoors.

» Become accustomed to riding the distance of the race prior to race day.

BEGINNER CYCLIST FAQS

What about clip-in shoes? To clip in or not to clip in, that is the question. At a local sprint you'll find that many riders use run shoes to carry them through the bike and the run legs. (Benefit: You save time during transition!) If using clip-ins sounds daunting, then I would recommend sticking with flat pedals during your first race. If you do want to make the switch now, then the key is to practice and practice some more! Here are a few steps to getting started:

» Hit a local bike shop to talk about pedal and bike shoe combinations and let them install your cleats.

» If possible, practice clipping in and out in an indoors situation first. If you have a trainer, then that's an easy way to do it. After you've got the hang of that, move on to the next step.

» A grassy field or parking lot is a great place to practice clipping in and out while moving. One thing to know: You will fall! It's inevitable, so pick somewhere with a soft surface if you can. The upside is that you should get the hang of clipping in and out quickly.

What kind of bike will athletes use at the race? The answer is all kinds: mountain bikes, commuter bikes, road bikes, and fancy bikes with disc wheels. My standard recommendation is to use whatever bike you have, or have access to, during your first tri. This includes borrowing a bike from someone.

Do I have to invest in cycling clothes? A pair of bike shorts or triathlon shorts can go a long way toward enhancing riding comfort. Both types of shorts have a pad that's designed to make riding more comfortable. Tri shorts have a thinner pad and can be worn through the swim, bike, and run legs. While some bike shorts have a pad that can be worn during the swim, most are used only for cycling.

What about pumping up tires? Tires need to be pumped before each and every ride. The proper PSI (pounds per square inch) should be displayed on the outside of your tire.

What about changing a tube? You should learn how to change your own tire and to have the proper equipment to do so. Visit your local bike shop and purchase a flat kit and saddle bag (a small pouch that can you hang under your saddle and carry your flat kit in). Ask the bike shop if they will demo changing a flat or see if they know of any upcoming tire change clinics. After watching, practice at home, preferably multiple times. Practice periodically to keep your skills sharp.

Do I really have to pick up bottles or food during the race? Anything that necessitates removing one hand from the handlebars seems intimidating at first. For safety reasons (and for staying hydrated), it is very important to practice this skill. If you're nervous, a good way to start is simply to practice removing one hand from the handlebars, then the other, for 5 or 10 seconds at a time. Force yourself to repeat this each time you ride and work up to where you can comfortably remove one hand for 30 seconds at a time. After you get the hang of it, practice taking your bottles out of the bottle cage or reaching into your pocket for a gel. Note: The key to doing this successfully is to be able to do it without taking your eyes off the road.

BEYOND BEGINNER CYCLING

After you've been riding for a while, you may find that you've stopped seeing quick progress. Here are some ideas to up the ante with your training:

Ride more—Sometimes the simplest solution is the best. If you've just started training in the last year or have taken a long break, simply ride more often. Make it fun by joining a group, trying out some software, or signing up for a fall century.

Get specific—Try structured training to help you break past your rut. If you're not up for hiring a coach or building a plan yourself, you can try out one of the plans available on TrainerRoad.com or Zwift.com.

Get a group—Riding with faster friends is a good way to push yourself out of your comfort zone. Ask your local bike shop or triathlon club about group rides.

Get help—After training diligently for a few years, further positive adaption requires more. Try a focused plan or hire a coach and be clear about your goals.

Check on details—Don't forget the details, like getting a professional bike fit or making sure you have the best bike for your body and budget.

An inevitable part of training is braving your first visit to the bike shop. They can be intimidating places. The employees are mostly male, they seem to know everything about bikes, and they're not impressed when you say you need a thingamajig. Here, Coach Kathryn gives tips for braving the shop for the very first time, for purchasing your first bike, and for regular maintenance.

#TriLessons: Braving the Bike Shop

—By Kathryn Taylor

I absolutely hate getting my car serviced. I will ignore the little service light as long as I possibly can and go in ready for whatever "upsell" the shop is going to try to give me. I felt that way for years until I finally found a shop run by a woman. She was always very upfront with me and didn't pressure me into buying new tires every time I walked in the door.

For many women, the bike shop feels similar to a used car lot or car service center. Most bike shops are run by people who are passionate about cycling and want to help, but because the whole process is new to first-timers, it still feels overwhelming. A little education goes a long way in feeling more comfortable when you walk into the store.

Tips for Buying a Bike

Clearly communicate when you walk in the door. This means you know your budget and how you plan to use this bike. If you want a bike for casual riding on the weekend with your husband, that's going to look different than a bike for the goal of doing an Ironman.

You also need to understand the cost of the bike is "as is." Factor in the cost for pedals, shoes, a new saddle (the ones that come on the bikes are almost never the right one), and a variety of other accessories. Estimate an additional $300 to $500 on top of the cost of the bike for those items.

When you walk in, introduce yourself to the salesperson and tell them how you plan to use the bike and what your budget range will be. They'll likely start throwing out a lot of terms that you aren't familiar with, so stop them with any question you may have.

Ask them about their bike fit process. Getting the right fit is going to be key to how you feel on the bike. If you can find a store with a Retull or GURU bike fitter, it's worth the investment. A bike fit should not just be a few measurements but should be a process of looking at your body and figuring out what bike works best for you. You can't always take a set of numbers and use it to purchase a bike.

You should understand two things about bike shops. First, most people who work in bike shops really love bikes. Like, they really love them. They are passionate about the very best bike. If you go in with no budget, they're always going to show you the top of the line bike anyway. There are lots of nice things about some of those bikes, but as a coach once told me, "it's the engine, not the bike." I've seen people have really great races on what some would consider very low-end bikes, and I've seen people have really terrible races on what would be considered a top of the line bike. Focus more on your training and less on all the awesome bike components that someone says will make you faster.

The second thing to understand is that there are a lot of rules that bike shops have to comply with, and these rules come from their distributors. The distributors will dictate when bikes can go on sale and for how much. Bikes are kind of like cars—the new models start to come out in November or December for the next year, and that's when you can often find the best deal on an older model bike. Distributors will allow for discounted rates.

If you find a bike on sale but it's not your size, ask if they can order it. Often suppliers will have extra in stock, but the bike shop is wanting to sell inventory on their floor. Be willing to walk away. It can feel emotional at the time, but it's okay to take a few days to shop around.

Tips for Getting Bike Service
It's important to establish a relationship with a bike mechanic that you trust. It's inevitable that right before a big ride or race, something will go wrong with your bike. You want to know that you have a person you can go to.

In my early days of triathlon, I bought a bike that didn't fit well at a store that was focused on sales. Every time I took my bike in for service, I felt like the mechanics were too busy to talk to me or treated me like I was dumb because I didn't know how to adjust my rubbing brake or fix my flat tire. So I avoided the bike shop until I was riding the trainer one day and my bike tire blew. Yep, that can happen. It sounds like a gunshot and will scare the bejeezus out of you. It was the day before a big bike ride, and I needed a mechanic. Out of desperation I tried my local shop, and I'm glad I did. I met Chris and he became my mechanic for several years.

What was different about Chris is he never treated me like I was dumb. He always took time to explain things. When he said I needed a tune-up, he'd explain why. He also wouldn't try to upsell me on services I didn't need. He knew my bike and its story, and when I would walk in with the bike, he would ask me about my latest race or what I was up to these days. I actually looked forward to going to his shop. You may need to shop around for the right mechanic. Just find the person that you feel comfortable with.

Learn to do it yourself. Too many triathletes get really intimidated by their bikes. You don't need to learn to be a full-service mechanic, but you should learn some basics like how to change your tire, how to adjust your brakes, how to fix a dropped chain, how to lube your chain, and how to clean your bike. Some bike shops will offer classes to teach these things, and there is a plethora of YouTube videos on the subjects. Practice these things until you feel comfortable with them. You'll feel much more comfortable out on the road knowing that you can handle any minor repairs that may happen.

17

RUN TRAINING

After finishing the Navy Seal Fitness Challenge, I signed up for my first marathon a mere four months away. Although my preparation was far from ideal, it had improved from my college efforts. Buoyed by progress from training regularly, I stuck to my training plan and even worked up to a few 20-mile runs!

Finally, the day arrived. It was humid and windy and rainy, a non-record-setting marathon day in an objective sense. Yet I was undeterred. I had an ambitious "A" goal I was embarrassed to say aloud. I started with a pace group, but didn't wear the bib on race morning. I imagined other athletes looking me up and down like "yeah right, she thinks she can run that fast?" Or worse, what if I slowed substantially, and my pace group finished 20 minutes ahead of me? "Aww good job," the spectators would say with pity in their eyes, as I shuffled to a finish, my bib proclaiming exactly how far I had fallen. So instead I lurked on the fringe of the pace group, one foot in, one foot out.

Running happy at my favorite local tri, the John Tanner Sprint Triathlon, in 2017

The pacer started fast, chatting along the way. We were banking time for sure, but "banking" is not generally a good strategy. Our pacer dutifully picked up gels for us when there was a stop. He had yelling conversations with other pacer friends as they headed the other way.

After a while, the wind picked up, and it started raining. One by one, our little crew started dropping off. By this time, we were a few minutes ahead of our stated goal. It was warm, and did I mention our pacer was pacing too fast? And boy did he talk a lot.

My calf muscle, which had given me trouble in training, started hurting more and more. It felt like it was literally ripping. I ignored it and figured I'd deal with the fallout later.

When we passed a group going the other way, our pacer had a moment of panic. "We took a wrong turn!" he screamed, taking the whole group on an immediate 180-degree turn. A mutiny was brewing. Some of the group refused to turn, and others were too exhausted to do anything other than follow blindly (like me).

After a couple of minutes our pacer realized we had been going the right way the first time. So we all turned around again. Now there were only eight of so of us left, and we were five minutes behind pace.

He tried to "catch us up," but the damage was already done. We were totally wiped, and I'm pretty sure no one actually finished up with the pacer. I did not end up reaching my time goal that day, but I did end up tearing my calf. And, I ended up learning a couple of important lessons:

» **Run your own race.** Whether it's a marathon or a 5K, someone running the same time goal is unlikely to pace the exact same way. Maybe they're a better hill runner or maybe they're more efficient on the downhill portion of the run.

» **Always know the course.** Easy to say, but hard for us directionally challenged folks to do. Still, it is technically the athlete's responsibility to know the course.

» **Don't stick your safety pin through a disposable timing chip.** After all that effort my first marathon didn't even "count." They eventually gave me credit online, but for a long time I was shown as a big fat DNF!

BEGINNER RUNNER DOS AND DON'TS

One of the great things about running is that it's so simple. Grab some shoes, and you're ready to go! If you haven't been running on a regular basis, start by using run–walk intervals to safely take you from walking the distance to running the distance.

Here are a few dos and don'ts to keep in mind as you get started.

DO UTILIZE PROPER FREQUENCY.

Run frequently to make it a habit and then a lifestyle. If you only run one to two times a week, you may never improve much, enjoy running, or experience many of the other benefits "they" talk about (like a runner's high).

I am reminded of this every time I am forced to take a break. Within a week, I recall why people say they can't stand running. It's because it feels terrible when you rarely run.

DO USE METRICS.

Use metrics to quantify your intensity. It's easy to fall into a trap of running as hard as you can every single run or running at a medium effort all the time. Neither of these are the best path to improvement.

DON'T CHASE DAILY PRS.

One common mistake most new runners make is to go for a PR—in distance or speed—each time they lace up their shoes. Eventually this approach will lead to injury and limit your ability to progress and thus improve.

RUNNING HURDLES TO TACKLE

SHOULD I USE PACE OR HEART RATE?

As a new runner, you may wonder whether you should use pace or heart rate when training and racing. The answer is: It depends.

Pace is considered the gold standard of run effort measurement because it is truly objective. Heart rate is a subjective measure of how your body is responding to the effort level. Used together, pace and HR can help you achieve success in pacing your race. But...shouldn't pace and heart rate zones track together? Not always. Let's review a few times where you would want to differentiate between pace and heart rate as drivers of training.

The Easy Run—On a hot summer's day, your pace may very well be zone 2 while your heart rate is zone 3 and beyond. This is a situation where I advise my athletes to look at heart rate as the primary driver. If you are constantly running at a high heart rate to hit an arbitrary pace on easy days, then you'll be too worn out to hit your quality workouts.

Summer Easy Run Tip: The idea of an easy day is that it's truly easy, so don't get caught up in worrying about what your easy pace was during the cooler months!

The Track—Besides the treadmill, the track is the closest we have to all factors being equal—it's flat, and it's a standard length. This is why it's the preferred place to run set distance intervals with pace as a primary driver.

Summer Track Tip: Start early. Start earlier than the time that just popped in your head. If the goal is to hit the pace, then you want to make it as easy for yourself as possible, which means running in the coolest part of the day, early morning or late evening.

The Long Run—If you're training for a half or full marathon, your key long runs will likely include some miles at race pace. For these runs, consider using a mix of heart rate and pace to execute your long run. For instance, if you are targeting a 13-mile long run with the last three miles at race pace, run the first 10 by heart rate (i.e., at an easy pace). That way when it's time to ramp it up, you won't already be exhausted from arbitrarily trying to hit a pace in the beginning.

Summer Long Run Tip: Don't make the mistake of running long in the middle of the day "for heat acclimation." Doing shorter, easier, or occasional workouts in the heat is heat acclimation. Performing key workouts in the heat is self-defeating overkill.

When you first start running, every other run is a distance or pace PR, and it's easy to get caught up in racing or going medium hard for each run. Many athletes become overly concerned with their speed and unconsciously develop rules related to pace:

"I don't like any of my runs to be slower than a 10-minute mile." "I refuse to walk during a run, even if my heart rate gets out of the prescribed zone." Those thought patterns can lead to burnout, lack of progress, and even injury.

But it's hard to forget about pace, especially if you're competitive with yourself. For this reason, ignoring pace and running by heart rate is a simple but powerful strategy. Consider ignoring pace and using heart rate instead during easy runs, triathlon races, and hot weather.

If you've set your running heart rate and pace zones in the past, then read on. If not, visit Joe Friel's Lactic Threshold Heart Rate primer (www.joefrielsblog.com/2010/05/quick-guide-to-training-with-heart-rate-power-and-pace.html) and make sure you're using accurate zones as a starting point.

BEGINNER RUNNER BEST PRACTICES

» Be willing to let go of your primary sport just a little bit.

» Practice good frequency from the beginning. Ten miles divided into three or four runs per week is much better than ten miles divided into two runs.

» Don't skimp on footwear.

» Don't go the same intensity all the time.

» Go easy on the easy days so you can go hard on the hard days.

QUICK STEPS TO START RUNNING

» Invest in proper footwear selected with expert help.

» Start where you are. If you've been sedentary, start with a walk-to-run program.

» Gradually build up volume and distance, being sure to progress no further than about 10% a week.

BEGINNER RUNNER FAQS

Does everyone run the entire race? No. There are many walkers, run/walkers, as well as those who walk the transitions as part of their race strategy.

How can people say they enjoy running? Commit to a six-week beginner plan, even if you hate it. Remember that just like anything else, there will be days you don't want to get out there, even if you technically enjoy it. You may be surprised at how much you enjoy running once you start doing it more regularly.

What if I really, really don't want to run? Many successful exercisers use a strategy of committing to start only. For example, say one day you're scheduled for a three-mile run, you may commit to just getting dressed for the run and getting through five minutes. Likely after that short period of time, you'll find the courage and motivation to keep going.

BEYOND BEGINNER RUNNING

Of the training tenets you can manipulate—volume, intensity, duration, and frequency—one of the most underrated and underutilized variables, in my opinion, is frequency. Many triathletes fall into the trap of infrequent runs that are then too intense or long for their training to support.

A common example is the athlete who will do a very long run on the weekend and perhaps one other tempo to all-out run during the week and call it good. This stunts progress and often leads to injury. Don't let this happen to you. Increase your run durability by practicing proper frequency.

Here are some tips for improving your run:

» **Increase frequency**—If you're currently a student of the run twice a week group, then build up your frequency slowly.

» **Intensity**—After you've built up frequency, then add in some intensity. An easy way to add in intensity is to run once a week with others who are slightly faster. Less is more here. You're likely also getting intensity from swim and bike workouts, so you need less quality (speedwork or hills) than you would as an open runner.

» **Set midterm goals**—Stay motivated and track your progress with periodic winter races. Targeting an off-season PB in 5K, 10K, or even half marathon will set you up to start the season off strong.

» **Consider joining a group**—Solo, near daily runs can get boring.

» **Consider hiring a coach**—A good coach can evaluate your strengths and weaknesses and recommend a personalized approach to attack your run. Video analysis can be a great tool to identify your strength and flexibility limiters.

#TriLessons:
Tips for the Runner Turned Triathlete

If you identify primarily as a runner who does triathlons, you may be concerned with keeping up your run performances while also training for triathlon. The good news is, this can be done. However, there are several common mistakes runners often make along the way.

Infrequent Running
Yes, I sound like a broken record, but it's that important. Cut back volume—if necessary—before frequency. Take your current mileage and divide it by four or five runs a week. That workload compared with taking your current mileage and dividing by two will take you a lot farther.

Fix It: Don't have time to run so much? Run more without adding much extra time to your training by inserting a short run after almost every cycle session.

Too Much Hard Running
Oftentimes "just running" is the goal. Many runners have misplaced pride in their paces .Or they feel they're not getting a

"good workout" unless they're huffing and puffing. Too much intensity on a daily basis has a major downside—it won't allow you to reach the levels you need to reach on the hard days.

Fix It: If you're a social runner and your training partners run too fast, consider running solo on easy days. If you're not sure how *easy* easy means, perform a heart rate test, then use those values to hold yourself back. If your propensity to run a certain pace is more of a pride thing, log a couple of 20-minute mile walks in Strava, and you'll soon realize nothing bad happens when you do.

Too Much Focus on "Speedwork"
A lot of triathlon running is really just running. Sure, you need some quality runs, but assuming you're doing some quality bikes and swims, too, most of your runs should truly be easy.

Fix It: Pick your quality workout(s) ahead of time, whether it be track, hill repeats, or a tempo run, and strictly hold yourself to running intensity during that workout only.

18

TRANSITION TRAINING

When Michelle Crossman left the bike to run transition—called T2—she was prepared. Really prepared. She sat down in transition, took the time to put on bike shorts, and reapplied sunscreen. When all was said and done, Michelle received the dubious distinction of the slowest transition in the entire race. Eight minutes!

Many years later, Michelle remembers her first tri experience fondly, and her first transition makes a fun story during beginner seminars. Since transitions are a timed part of the race experience, we would be remiss if we did not cover them in this book. Transitions *can* seem complicated, but breaking them down and then practicing makes them simple.

A typical transition setup. Bonus points if you can identify what's wrong in this picture.

BEGINNER TRANSITION DOS AND DON'TS

DON'T BRING TOO MANY THINGS.

Too many choices make it tough to do things quickly and efficiently. As a beginner, don't fall into the trap of bringing far too many items to transition. In our tri club, we have a handy towel listing everything you need in a transition. I still use this towel each race.

Here are the items listed on the towel:

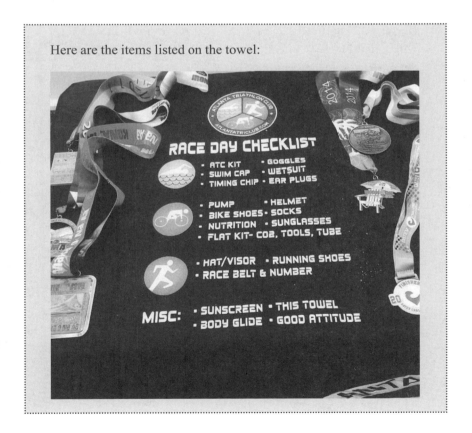

Fix It: See the towel list in the figure and don't bring anything besides what's on that list, including a bucket! If you're worried about needing extra stuff, leave it in the car so you won't be tempted to rifle through it during the race.

DO (MENTALLY) MARK YOUR SPOT.

In the common concerns chapter, I mentioned my own transition fumble, losing my bike. The prevailing advice when I started was to put a balloon near your spot or mark the ground with chalk. If you do a few races, you'll realize that some of those things will actual block or interfere with other competitors, which you definitely don't want to do.

A less complicated way to mark your spot is to look for natural landmarks like a tree, flag, or trash can. Plot your spot on an imaginary axis. This landmark denotes my x axis, and this is my y access. This will allow you to find your spot coming from different directions.

Fix It: Walk through transition prior to the race and practice approaching your spot from different directions. This is best done after you set up your transition spot and right before the race starts so the information will be fresh in your mind.

DON'T DO THINGS STATIONARY THAT CAN BE DONE WHILE MOVING.

Putting on your hat. Putting on your race belt. Eating a sandwich. These things can all be done while running or walking rather than while you're stationary.

Fix it: Practice efficient movement with everything that "has" to be done stationary—for example, putting on your shoes. Plan strategies to make movements more efficient—for example, clipping together your visor and race belt so you can grab them and run.

DON'T GIVE YOURSELF TOO MANY CHOICES.

Do you want a strawberry gel or a vanilla one? The time to make the decision is prior to your race. Leaving yourself exactly one option can really help speed things up.

Fix It: Make the decisions prior to transition close time and stick to it.

DO KNOW THE RULES.

Did you know your transition setup should be by your front wheel? And that you must wait to mount your bike until after the mount line? Knowing the rules beforehand can mitigate stress on race day! We'll cover some rules in the race day section, but visit USA Triathlon to see a complete list: www.teamusa.org/USA-Triathlon/About/Multisport/Competitive-Rules/Most-Common-Rules-Violations.

Fix It: Spend a few minutes re-reviewing rules prior to race day, and you should be all set! Experienced triathletes are always happy to help a newbie on race day.

THE IMPORTANCE OF PRACTICE

Practicing the bike to run transition is easy. As a part of your training, simulate your bike transition—T1—at least once a week.

Swim to bike transition—T2—is more of a logistical challenge. If the site where you'll be open water swimming has a small area where you can cycle afterwards, it's a worthwhile thing to try it out.

In an attempt to simplify the steps needed to transition, use these tips:

GENERAL SETUP TIPS

» The less gear you have the better. Don't give yourself too many options (i.e., will I feel like a strawberry gu or a chocolate one?).

» Prior to the race, practice approaching your bike in transition from swim and then again from the bike. Identify a landmark if possible.

» Lay your gear out on the towel in the order in which you'll use it. For example, bike shoes go in front of run shoes.

» Put your transition bag back in the car or get it out of the way by placing it against the fence. The space under the bikes is crowded enough without a bunch of bags jammed in there.

TERMS TO KNOW

Mount and Dismount Line—Imagine how chaotic it would be if everyone rode their bikes in the actual transition area. To avoid this scenario and keep things fair, there is a mount/dismount line immediately outside of transition. You must run or walk your bike past this line before mounting at the beginning of the bike leg. After returning from the bike leg, you must dismount before this line before entering transition. The line is clearly marked and usually has multiple volunteers stationed there to remind riders.

STEPS TO T1

1. When you get out of the lake or pool, keep swimming until your hand hits the bottom of the lake or you touch the wall. Don't waste energy and time by switching from swimming to walking too soon.

2. Stand up. You did it! Now think about the steps of transition as you walk or run to the transition spot. You already practiced finding your transition spot, so you should know what it looks like from this angle.

3. While walking or running, peel down your wetsuit or speedsuit to your hips, if wearing one. Do this before taking off your goggles and swim cap and hold them in your dominant hand.

4. As you run, think through the steps of your transition.

5. Once you reach your spot, finish taking off your wetsuit or speedsuit and throw down your goggles and cap. Put on your helmet and fasten it first, then put on your bike shoes. If wearing sunglasses, put those on and, if carrying extra nutrition, put that in your pocket. Now grab your bike and walk or run toward the exit. That's it!

STEPS TO T2

1. Consume remaining nutrition in the last few miles of the bike.

2. Dismount your bike before the dismount line and think about the steps of transition as you run or walk your bike to your transition spot.

3. Mount bike on the rack first, then then remove your helmet and bike shoes.

4. Put on running shoes and socks, if needed. (T2 is where I put on my socks for distances longer than a sprint.)

5. Grab your race number and belt that's clipped around your visor or hat. You can put these items on while walking or running. Grab nutrition, if needed, on the way out.

BEGINNER TRANSITION FAQS

Socks or No Socks? Going without can save time but if you end up with massive blisters, it's a net loss. Practice if you intend to try it. Many experienced triathletes have a distance breakpoint after which they wear socks. For example, I don't wear socks for a sprint-distance race, but I wear them during the run for longer distances.

Where does my stuff go? Your transition setup goes by your front wheel of your bike when racked by the seat.

What about a pump? Most larger races will have a bike shop supporting with pumps or an air compressor. If in doubt, bring your own. If you bring your bike on race day and park on site, pump your tires at your car.

Can I leave my bike pump or bag in transition? This varies. Check out specific rules for your race prior to the day.

Where can I go to the bathroom? There are generally porta-potties in transition as well as at each aid station on the run course.

Can I change? Nudity is not allowed during transition. In smaller races, there isn't a place to change, so if at all possible, you should wear the same clothes from start to finish. In IRONMAN races, there are gender-specific changing tents, and you can change after each leg if desired.

What are T1, T2, and T3? T1 is the swim to bike transition. T2 refers to the bike to run transition. T3 refers to the afterparty that immediately follows the race.

What's a race belt? A race belt is essentially a piece of elastic that clips around your hips and holds your number. Since most races only require wearing your number during the run, it's impractical to wear it the whole race.

BEYOND BEGINNER TRANSITIONS

» Consider going without socks (practice first). A little Vaseline or Bodyglide around areas of potential chafe can help prevent blisters.

» Run the entire way through transition. Don't dawdle.

» There should be no sitting at any point.

» Practice (and execute) flying dismounts. Flying mounts don't save time unless done well (because of time wasted fumbling with feet in shoes). But dismounts, which allow running through transition sans bike shoes, definitely do. Search YouTube for more tips on these two skills.

» Clip your visor/hat to your race belt so you can put on both while running.

» If wearing a wetsuit, use Bodyglide or other lubricant around your ankles and lower legs so you can slide it off more quickly.

19

TACKLING NUTRITION

Everyone has an opinion about nutrition and much of the advice—even from experts—seems to conflict. Should you eat high carb for energy? Low carb and teach yourself to burn fat? Something else entirely?

Here Ilana Katz, MS, RD, CSSD gives us the lowdown on training and racing nutrition. "Think about a lifestyle versus a plan. If you can't envision yourself sticking with your plan a year from now, then it's not a lifestyle choice."

Ilana defines good nutrition as meeting your daily caloric needs and giving your body what it needs to perform daily processes. In the case of the athlete, you also need a little bit extra for your body to use during exercise and to repair and rebuild afterward. She emphasizes that there is no set philosophy that works for everyone, and that different plans fit different lifestyles.

DAILY NUTRITION

As a new athlete training for a shorter distance race, keep things simple and avoid major changes on race day. Here are some of Ilana's tips for daily nutrition:

» Minimize processed food.

» Reduce simple sugars.

» Focus on healthy fats (omega, poly-, and monounsaturated) versus saturated or trans fats.

» Include lots of color and fiber.

» Eat foods that come from the earth.

BEGINNER NUTRITION FAQS

Should I Eat Breakfast? Yes. Eating breakfast revs up your metabolism, especially if you eat within 30 minutes of waking.

What does "keep food clean" mean? Dump the bars, the cereal, and things that come in a package. Question the claims written on the box as they are often misleading. Speaking of boxes, there's really no food you need that comes in a box. Try to stick to eating nutrient-dense food (rich in color and fiber) versus calorie-dense food with limited nutrients (such as sodas, fast food, and candy).

How many times should I eat a day? The body stores carbs in limited amounts; therefore, eating smaller meals more often throughout the day will help maintain well-fueled muscles. Eating just one or two big meals a day can actually slow down the metabolism.

How many servings of fruits and vegetables should I eat? Eat lots of fruit and vegetables throughout the day. These superfoods are high in antioxidants which combat the buildup of free radicals from exercise, as well as high in vitamins and minerals that keep your metabolic pathways working efficiently and effectively. They are also the perfect example of high-density nutrition (low calorie but full of nutrients).

What's the best way to stay on track? Whether your goal is weight loss, performance, maintenance, or greater focus on the right kinds of food, keeping a food log can help. Patterns provide valuable data that can help you get to the root of a problem. Furthermore, logs make you accountable to your goals and your current focus.

TRAINING NUTRITION TIPS

If your daily nutrition is on point, then you should not worry much about training and racing nutrition unless you move up to longer distances. That said, here are some basic tips from Ilana:

» Rev up your metabolism by eating within 30 minutes of waking up, even if its pre-workout. If you have a hard time eating before a workout, start off with half a banana to get used to it; its easily digestible, high in carbs, and low in fiber, which contribute to a more efficient workout.

245

» Use protein as part of the recovery meal. It begins the rebuild and recovery of muscles and helps you feel more satisfied, decreasing the temptation to overeat after many hours of intense activity.

» Recover with a 3:1 carb to protein ratio after your workout as soon as possible—preferably within 30 minutes. One example is a protein shake with one scoop of protein, one to two servings of fruit, and some fresh spinach or greens blended together. Others include low-fat chocolate milk or a ready-made protein drink for convenience.

» Sports nutrition has many individual facets. Therefore, always have a sports nutrition strategy for training and racing. Plan in segments. How many grams of carbs per mile or per 30-minute block of time? Plan textures and products, such as liquids (GatoradeT, accelerade T), solids (sports beans, shot bloks), or semi-solids (gels).

» Know your carbs and fuel accordingly. Pre-workout and post-workout carbs can be higher in Glycemic Index (GI) compared to the rest of the meals in a day, where slower burning carbs would be more appropriate. If you are not sure of the different fuel burning rate of carbs, good examples of fast are sports drinks, gels, and shot bloks, also bananas and potatoes. Slower burning would be whole-grain products, whole grains themselves (like brown rice, barley, quinoa), legumes, and oats (more fibrous carbs slow the fuel burn rate).

» Stay hydrated. The goal before your workout is to be hydrated; the goal during your workout is to replace losses; and the goal after a workout is to rehydrate and replenish electrolytes from sweat loss. A basic rule of thumb for daily hydration is to drink half your body weight in liquid ounces.

» Experiment with nutrition during training. Never try new products during a race and stick to your plan.

RACING NUTRITION FAQS

Should I carbo load? An athlete racing a sprint triathlon or a 5K does not need to carbo load. Daily nutrition will suffice. However, if racing a marathon or a longer triathlon, you may wish to experiment with carbo loading. Use safe and effective carbo-loading strategies, starting about a week before a race. Tapering exercise and switching carbs to a higher percentage at least two to three days before a race leading up to the race is the most effective way of carbo loading. Do not overeat the night before or the early morning before a race.

How should I time my race day eating? It is preferable to have a consistent strategy of intake, in other words not to have big gulps of sports drink/water or chunks of food all at once when you feel hungry or thirsty. You should have a strategy that allows you to feel comfortable eating every 30 to 40 minutes. Some athletes even prefer 15- to 20-minute intervals (much of this is based on your own gut and how well you can handle sports products).

How should I time pre-race (or pre-workout) intake? Give yourself enough time for your food to digest. The more fiber, fat, or protein you consume, the longer you need for digestion. Quick burning carbs (closer to simple sugars) can be taken as close as 20 to 30 minutes before the race (e.g., white potato, banana, or white bread). If the carbs have fiber such as oats or whole-grain breads, give yourself at last an hour for digestion.

Preferably start your sports nutrition intake with 15 to 20 minutes of the time you are physically active and then be consistent as to your formula of calories per hour. Humans typically oxidize 60 g of carbs per hour (there are 4 cal per g of carb, so that equals 240 cal per hour); if you break that up into 30-minute periods, it means an intake of 30 g or 120 cal per half hour, consistently.

At what point (length of workout) should I start supplementing? Workouts over 90 minutes do require a replenishment of glycogen during the workout; however, start the fueling process early (within 20 minutes). Do not wait until the 90 minutes is over to start fueling long workouts. Utilize sports nutrition during any training session over one hour, which enables them to train their gut to digest necessary carbs at higher heart rates. It may not be necessary for every short workout, but just like one trains their aerobic or musculoskeletal system, one can also train their gastrointestinal system for endurance.

Where should I start in terms of calories per hour? On average, start at 240 to 300 cal per hour (based on an average human oxidation rate of 1 g of carbs per minute). Many factors influence this amount, including size (more mass requires more calories), sweat rate, rate of glycogen depletion, fitness levels (many ironman athletes train their gut to handle closer to 300 and more calories per hour). Again, optimal consumption is very individual.

WHAT'S YOUR WORST RACE DAY NUTRITION MISTAKE?

» *"The day before IM Boulder, I had tacos from a food truck... by that night I had a slight case of food poisoning. Up all night in the bathroom and almost DNS the next morning. I powered through, but it was ugly. My longest IM and the only race I've done that I can say I stopped at every port-a-potty on the bike and run course. Don't eat from street vendors and food trucks the day before an Ironman."* – Kelly

» *"I had a beer handed to me at mile 26 of the marine corps marathon—almost had to walk up the last .2 because I felt sick. That was not smart."* – Clare

#TriLessons: Most Important Training Sessions Prior to Race Day

For any beginner seeking her first finish line, the most important part of training is developing the endurance to get to the finish line safely. Remembering this principle can help you prioritize when training isn't going perfectly. And when does it ever?

In an ideal world, you will complete 90% of everything on your schedule; however, sometimes this isn't realistic. You may worry that you haven't done enough training to finish. You hate to ask this question, but if you have to cut sessions, where should your priorities lie?

Don't skip the (weekly extra) session in your weakest sport—Most of us have our weak leg, a.k.a., our "third best sport." Consider those training sessions the most important ones on your schedule. For many "adult onset" swimmers, that workout is often the swim. But it can also be the bike or run. The ironic thing is your "third best" sport sessions are the ones easiest to skip. Don't fall into this trap, but make those workouts must-dos.

Don't forget a swim lesson or clinic—Since successful swimming is so technique oriented, a swim lesson or clinic to target stroke flaws is a must for newbie swimmers. Whatever habits you ingrain at the start of your swim "career" will be extremely tough to break later. Particularly if you're a new or nervous swimmer, sign up for a few one-on-one lessons, then commit to practicing your drills and swimming three times a week for the duration of the training period.

Don't leave out (multiple) open water swims—Swimming in the pool is different than swimming in open water. Practice as many times as possible. Make it happen, even if it involves a long drive and inconvenience.

Don't neglect frequent sessions—To save time, perform more frequent, short sessions rather than skimping on the absolute number of sessions each week. Take the example of running. If you're going to run, say, 15 miles per week, split those miles into four or five runs versus running once or twice. Frequency improves durability and is the first step to improving your running. Running easy (and frequently) before any long runs should be added and certainly before adding intensity (like track) into your program.

Don't forget fueling—It doesn't have to be complicated. Keep it simple for your first and make sure you're having some sort of quick-energy, high-carbohydrate snack and fluid with electrolytes during the race. An example for a sprint triathlon would be a bottle of water with a nuun tablet and a gel consumed during the bike portion.

Part Four
Get Set

Congrats! You've
made it through
training, now it's
time for race day.

In this section,
we'll talk about
the weeks leading
up to race day
as well as the event.

#TriLesson: The Mental Side of Race Day

Every first-timer receives advice about getting to transition early, not starting out too hard, and managing race nutrition. But what about your motivation, your mental game? What should you think about when the going gets tough? In other words, a mantra. An athlete and friend of mine, Kelsey, swears by "run like a magical little pixie fairy." Others have a song that always gets stuck in their head, or some even think of a friend or family member for inspiration. Here are a few of my favorite mid-race motivations:

Focus on process—Anything that keeps you in the present moment is good. For example, focusing on an aspect of your breathing or form. Personally, I like to plan a game called "swim machine" where the goal is not to break stroke during the swim. It sounds silly, but it helps me to think about the process—swimming continuously, one stroke at a time—rather than "am I going to hit a certain time goal" or "is someone going to whack me in the head."

Dangle a carrot—Promising yourself you can take a walk break at mile two doesn't sound like much, but riches are relative when you're racing. Keeping focused on the present, what you need to be doing, and in the time period just ahead can help your mind not become your worst enemy. Another way to trick yourself is to promise yourself you can do x, y, or z if you just get to a certain benchmark first. For this to work, the benchmark must be close. For example, I might tell myself that I'll stop pushing if I can just get to the top of a hill. Then once I crest, I'll pick a new spot to "slow down."

Use social motivation—Cheering for others will give them a boost, and it gives you one, too. When you're breathing hard, encouragement can be a small wave or a breathless "good job!"

Stay thankful—How often have you talked to friends after a race, and all they talk about is how they dropped their gel or got a cramp, and it screwed up everything. Lame! It's easy to fall into the trap of focusing on the negative, but it's a dangerous habit. Not only does it make you a downer to talk to, it also sets up a trap where you can never be happy after a race.

Fake it till you make it—It's natural to believe other people have some quality that you lack. But it's just not true. The chance that you are the *least* trained individual out of the 500 or 2,000 people racing is very small. I like to tell this one to my athletes because they've all been training hard. They've been training so hard that they've hired a coach! Therefore, not only are they not the least trained, they are likely among the most trained! Simple logic.

20

YOUR FIRST RACE

Michelle Crossman and her husband Ed decided to do a triathlon while driving home from their first obstacle race. After a day of mud, blood, and electrocution, Michelle decided to look for a different hobby. By the time they arrived home, she had successfully looked up and registered them for their very first sprint triathlon.

Their preparation started and ended there. A few weeks later at the sprint, Michelle found herself feeling frazzled and unprepared. First off, Michelle lost her goggles before the start and panicked. She ran around the race site frantically looking. Finally, she went to the bathroom and found the missing goggles on her head!

Things improved after the gun went off. After surviving the swim using only the breaststroke, Michelle sauntered into T1, looking around at other participants for tips. She pulled on wet bike shorts, which took a full minute in itself, and casually applied sunscreen. After leaving with her bike she had to come all the way back because she forgot a helmet. She ended up with the slowest T1 in the entire race.

After a successful bike ride, Michelle mounted up a Camelback for a two-mile run. Despite all this, she and Ed both crossed the finish line successfully. Immediately after—probably on the way home— they joined a club and signed up for an open water swim lesson.

Michelle learned a lot and modified her approach for her next race. Today, both Ed and Michelle are avid triathletes and triathlon coaches.

DOS AND DON'TS AS YOUR RACE APPROACHES

With your first race approaching, you may find yourself worrying about things you never considered. Should you finally figure out why your bike makes that squeaking noise? Do you need new shoes or is it already too late? Here is what needs to be accomplished in the weeks leading up to your race.

FOUR TO SIX WEEKS BEFORE YOUR RACE:

» Do practice all your race day details. Train in your race day attire, practice your hydration and nutrition, and make any last-minute purchases. If you need new shoes, then start breaking them in now.

» If you are staying in a hotel, do finalize your reservations and travel plans. Try to wrap up any other logistics so you won't have to stress about them last minute.

» Do get your bike tuned up and purchase gear needed to fix a mechanical issue, like a flat tire.

» Do practice transition. Practice the bike to run transition and practice swim to bike if feasible.

» Do consider volunteering at a local triathlon. Things you read about make more sense when seen in person.

» Don't make any equipment changes like a new saddle or bike fit. It will take weeks to get used to these changes.

» Do test your pre-race meal by eating then training at the same times you will on race day.

TWO WEEKS BEFORE YOUR RACE:

» Do taper according to your training plan. Depending on the length and type of event, start to reduce training in prep for a great race day performance. Follow your plan and don't attempt "just one more" long bike or run.

» Do practice transitions. If possible, practice a short workout on a lake or beach where you can complete swim, bike, and run plus transitions. At this point, the workout should not be a long session.

» Do a bike safety check. If you didn't go for a tune-up in the previous weeks, ensure breaks aren't rubbing, bolts aren't loose, and other safety basics. If bike maintenance is not your forte, enlist the help of a friend or bike shop. Be sure to plan ahead since many shops get swamped and don't take drop-ins during the season.

» Don't do anything new. A new pair of shoes, a different flavor of gel, a new bike position—you should avoid changes like these in the last few weeks before your race.

RACE WEEK

Race week is here! Nail race week so you can show up to the line and take best advantage of all your hard preparation:

» Do recognize ups and down are normal. Effects of your taper may include feeling great or feeling terrible. Do not worry if you feel a little extra grumpy, hungry, or anxious. It is totally normal. Do only what your plan calls for and nothing else. Doing too much this close to race day will only hurt you and not help you. If you are doing cross-training, such as strength training, consider dropping it the last week and a half prior to your race.

» Do follow your training plan. Your plan will have you reducing the volume of workouts while maintaining frequency and some intensity. Don't fall into the temptation of "one last big workout" the week of the race. It's too late to absorb your efforts, and this behavior will only make you tired on race day.

» Don't do nothing. You will not feel good with zero exercise. Ideally, your taper will include close to the same frequency of workouts with a reduction and volume and a sprinkling of intensity at race pace.

» Do read the athlete guide. When is bike drop-off? Can you pick up your packet on race morning? Plan ahead of time. In many smaller races, these can be done on race morning. However, I have also received a panicked call from an athlete late at night because they didn't know to drop their bike the day before the IRONMAN.

» Do attend pre-race meetings. Most races will have a meeting the day before the race or immediately prior to the start. In this meeting, they'll discuss important things like last-minute course changes, weather contingencies, or safety hazards. Always attend these meetings if possible.

» Don't try anything new physically. Now is not the time to take up CrossFit or switch to the keto diet. In general, try to keep variables the way you have been.

» Do get as much rest as possible in the last couple days before the race. If possible, try to avoid spending a lot of time walking around a crowded expo. If you're traveling to an out of town race, limit walking. Also, be cognizant of sleep. The sleep two nights before the race is the most important. It's normal to have trouble sleeping the night before the race, so don't worry if it happens to you.

» Do lay out everything you will need the morning of the race the night before. Make sure you have your number and timing chip if your race includes one. Relax and try to get off your feet.

> **WHAT IS "RACE AGE?"**
>
> Per USA Triathlon rules, athletes race against one another in five-year age categories. Your age is how old you'll be on December 31 of that year.

RACE DAY

All the work is done! A little anxiety is okay; it just means that you care!

WHAT TO DO ON RACE DAY

» **Pre-race meal**—At a minimum, eat your pre-race meal 90 minutes before the start. Keep the same rhythms you would on a normal training morning.

» **Get there early**—It's common to arrive to a triathlon two or even more hours earlier than the actual race start. Look at race rules to see what time transition opens and closes. Then, arrive early enough to have at least an hour in transition.

» **Bring everything**—Bring everything, then leave a lot of it in the car. Don't have too many choices in transition.

» **Pump your tires**—Tires need to be pumped to the recommended amount before every race and certainly on race day.

» **Rack your bike**—Bring your bike into transition. There will be stickers to place on your bike provided in your race packet, and they often have to be put on prior to entering. Rack your bike in the area indicated by race number. In many smaller races, the racks designate a range of numbers (e.g., 11-18), and you can rack anywhere in that range. The coveted spots are the ends because you have more room! If you get there early enough, you can nab one of these spots; if not, you can rack somewhere else. The bikes must be sorted end to tail in succession.

» **Body marking**—If number tattoos are not provided in your race packet, then volunteers will mark your arms and calves outside of transition with your race number and the age you'll be on December 31 of that year.

» **Set up transition**—Lay your towel by your front wheel. Try to take up minimal space. Organize everything into the order in which you'll use it.

» **Notice landmarks**—Find a few landmarks that designate your spot. Approach your spot from the directions you'll be coming from after the swim and the bike. Figure out where the swim entrance, bike in/out, and run out are located. They are generally large blowup arches and should be easy to spot from anywhere in transition.

» **Bring your swim stuff out**—Bring the stuff you need for the swim. A swim cap is provided in your packet and shows the wave you'll be starting in and what time. You'll also need goggles and a wetsuit if using one. Wetsuit legality, which is determined by temperature on race morning, will be announced—usually repeatedly—during transition.

» **Swim**—If allowed, take a quick swim and look back at landmarks to route you to the finish. Note: If the air is colder than about 60 degrees, I usually won't warm up the swim. If you aren't able to get in the water before the race, then stick your face in or splash water on your face. This also helps with acclimation.

TRANSITION CHECKLIST

Swim Gear:

» Attire (swimsuit or trisuit possibly covered by a wetsuit)

» Goggles

» Antifog

» Swim cap (provided by the race)

Bike Gear:

» Helmet (mandatory every time you're on your bike before during and after race)

» Bike shoes (if not wearing running shoes)

» Socks (optional)

» Sunglasses (optional)

» Water bottle(s)

> » Tire changing kit
>
> Running Gear:
>
> » Running shoes
>
> » Race number (attached to a race belt or to your attire)
>
> » Socks (optional)
>
> » Visor or hat (optional)

DECIPHERING YOUR RACE PACKET

Your race packet includes several things you'll need:

» **Race numbers**—In most races you'll receive a small sticker that goes on your bike stem, a larger one that goes around your seatpost or top tube, and another for your helmet. These stickers are required, and you should put on the bike stickers before entering transition.

» **Swim cap**—The swim cap is a color that designates your swim wave and start time. If this information is not on the race website, it should be available at check-in.

» **Timing chip**—Your timing chip will either be in your packet or available to pick up right by check-in. You must have a chip to receive an official time. It goes on your left ankle so it won't be a hazard on the bike.

» **Possibly tri tats**—Number tattoos may be in your packet, but in most smaller races, they'll use a sharpie.

SWIM START TERMINOLOGY

Wave start—Most local triathlons are wave starts. Typically, you will start with your age group (e.g., females 40-44). If it's a smaller race, there may be multiple groups starting in your wave.

Novice wave—Many local races have a novice wave that starts in the back of the swim, meaning less bodily contact. You can choose to race age group or novice when you sign up. Typically, after one to two races, it's no longer considered good form to register as a novice

Time trial start—If space is limited, as in a small lake or river, the race will sometimes do a time trial start. During these, racers line up and enter the water in quick succession a few seconds apart.

WHAT TO DO DURING THE RACE

The Swim

» Seed yourself properly—No matter where you start, expect a bit of contact. If you're primarily concerned about contact, then consider starting to one side or in the back. The most competitive swimmers will be looking to swim the straightest, shortest line to the buoys.

» Sight frequently—Every swimmer has had the experience of swimming off course. There will be volunteers in boats or kayaks along the way to ensure safety and to keep you from swimming too far afield.

» Consider waiting a few seconds to start—Again, if you're primarily concerned about avoiding contact, consider waiting about 10 seconds after the announcer says go.

» During your practice sessions, practice the breaststroke or flipping on your back as a measure to catch your breath—You can also grab a kayak if necessary. This will not result in disqualification as the swimmer isn't making forward progress.

» Go around the buoys—Generally, the turn buoys are mandatory, while the in-between ones are just suggestions.

» Take your time—There will be plenty of time to start strong and "race" the swim later if you desire. For your first, aim for a 3 out of 5 effort (see RPE scale).

Transition 1

» Right before you reach the shore, think about the steps involved in your transition.

» Keep swimming until your hand hits the beach. Swimming is faster than walking through deep water, so swim as long as you can.

» Unzip your wetsuit and pull it down to your hips as you run to your bike.

» Locate your bike by either finding your landmarks or counting the number of rows.

» Always put on your helmet first. Riding without a helmet before, during, or after a race is a potential DQ— disqualification.

TRANSITION 1 PRO TIPS

» Put your bike in an easy gear to start.

» If you're using socks, put them in your shoes and open ready to quickly slide on.

» If you're sliding your feet in your shoes, then make sure your shoelaces are loose enough to do so, or use speed laces.

» Loosen your cycling shoes so you can quickly slide your feet in.

» Attach your race belt (if using one) to your hat so you can grab and go while moving.

The Bike Ride

» Monitor your intensity—For an experienced racer, a sprint is a 4.5/5 effort. For your first, aim to start at a 3.5/5 effort. However, if it's your first time or your training has been inconsistent, pare back a gear or two below that.

» When you're climbing up a hill, shift so you're still maintaining cadence. You should never reach the top of the hill and have to stop pedaling to rest. If you do, then you've hit the hill too hard.

» Drink fluids throughout the ride and take calories if planned.

Transition 2

» Slow as you approach the dismount line.

» Rerack your bike in the same spot and in the same direction.

» Start out slow. Hopefully you've done some bricks, but your legs may still feel tight or shaky. Gradually ease into your pace.

» Run slightly easier than "you think you can."

» Try to maintain an even effort throughout the run instead of an even pace. That means slowing slightly on the uphills and pushing through on the downhills.

TRANSITION 2 PRO TIPS

» If you've practiced running without socks, slide your feet in, grab your hat and race number, and go!

» Don't do anything stationary you can do while moving. In T2, you only need to take off cycling shoes and put on run shoes while stationary.

Finish Line

» Smile for your finish line photo.

» Take in the moment. You've earned it!

FIRST RACE FAQS

Should I warm up? Warming up is recommended. A short walk/jog of about 10 minutes is a great way to warm up. Some races will allow you to get into the water prior to the race start. Take advantage of this if offered and go for a very short swim to loosen up. This will also allow you to check out landmarks for sighting.

How long should it take? Since race distances and experience levels vary, this is hard to say. One trick is to look at results from previous years on the race website.

Will I be pulled if I'm too slow? Check the race website for cutoff times on each leg. If you think you'll be close to cutoff times in any of the disciplines, consider emailing the race organizer to ask about how strictly they adhere to the posted time standards.

21

AFTER THE RACE

Post race involves several phases of acceptance. Phase one involves thinking, or saying, "I am *never* doing this again!" That phase can begin as early as during the actual race and usually continues immediately after. After a few hours, or days, this phase morphs into: "I am never doing that again. But if I *did,* I could do so much better…" During phase two, you think about what you could have done differently or better. In phase three, you think about trying some of those tweaks. What would happen if I trained the run more? What would happen if didn't stop so many times during the swim? In phase four, you're ready to sign up for your next challenge!

After you recover, keep the positive changes you've made by picking a new goal. Here are a few ideas:

Go faster—Pick a race similar to the one you just targeted. You completed a sprint, now it's time to complete one after more training with an eye toward improving your performance.

John and I finished Escape from Alcatraz within a few minutes of one another in 2015.

Go farther—If going farther sounds appealing, then consider stepping up the distance. Do you have what it takes to complete an Olympic-distance race? Perhaps you have a long-term goal of tackling the IRONMAN.

Go solo—Through your training journey, you may have found a knack for one of the sports and want to conquer a solo swim, bike, or run race.

Go social—Maybe you love the social environment and the camaraderie. If you haven't already, consider joining a tri club or other group in your area. Many athletes consider triathlon a lifestyle and participate in group workouts and activities with less focus on racing.

Go wide—If you don't have the desire to do another tri at this moment, use your newfound energy and motivation for something new. Maybe tri-ing gave you the confidence to finally switch careers, take that trip, or move.

#TriLessons: Carry the One

Whether you cross your first finish line and immediately sign up for ten races or hang up your bike to focus on other things, take what you've gained—energy, discipline, motivation, drive—and carry it with you wherever you go.

As an adult, life can seem like a list of endless obligations. Taking the steps to cross your first finish line gives you something that's just for you. It disrupts your routine; it makes you develop habits that support your goal; it makes you strive for more.

When I first discovered triathlon in 2009, I believed that I'd found it. You know, *it*, it. The thing that I'd be obsessed with forever, the target of all my meandering online searches, the thing I daydreamed about anytime I had a free moment.

Instead, while I still think triathlon is awesome (obviously), I believe it's true gift is allowing us to tap back into that childhood place where anything is possible, where hard work is play, and where effort is tied directly to reward.

Because triathlon may not be *the* thing, but the thing that leads to the thing. So wherever you go next, carry the one. Carry whatever you gained—life lessons, friendship, confidence, and more—along to life's next adventure. May it drive you to dreams and goals you never imagined before.

APPENDIX

TRAINING PLANS

Your beginner triathlon plan will have you swimming three times a week, cycling twice per week, and running twice a week plus one to two bricks. This plan is a very general framework. If you're already training more, then consider checking out the intermediate or advanced plan available at bethanyrutledge.com. If you're doing far less than the training in week one, you may need to bridge by practicing skills in all three sports before starting.

THE SWIM

Effort levels—Unless otherwise indicated, your swim warm-up and cool-down should always be easy (1 out of 5 on our RPE scale.) Unless otherwise indicated your main set effort level should be moderate (3 out of 5 on our RPE scale.) Practice bilateral breathing on every warm-up.

Before and after—You need a "before" to judge the success of your "after." This means taking a video of your stroke and testing a benchmark set before you start. Ideally, you'll kick off with a video analysis of your stroke from an experienced coach. Your second best option is to have a friend record a video of your swim. Even if you don't have someone to analyze your video, it can still be helpful to visualize your stroke. Often, what we think we're doing isn't actually what we're doing.

Test set—If possible, you should kick off with a test set so you have context by which to judge improvements. Your test set is as simple as performing a 50 and 100 for time.

» Easy 10-minute warm-up (mix of strokes and drills)

» 50 yards for time from a push start (rest for two minutes)

» 100 yards for time from a push start

» Cool-down to finish

DRILL IDEAS

You can perform any drills, but if you need ideas, here are a few of Megan Melgaard's favorites. Refer to bethanyrutledge.com or do an internet search for a video example of these drills.

Body position—Common issues are sinking legs, swimming uphill, and hips swinging from side to side. Focus on activating the core, maintaining proper head position (focus the gaze down), keeping leg position in relation to the surface (heels should breach the surface of the water when kicking), and rotating (shoulder and hip should rotate in line).

Best drill fix—Pulling with a buoy in between the ankles. Engage core to keep muscles activated and body streamlined. Add a snorkel to maintain proper head position.

Breathing—Common issues are holding the breath and exhaling when the mouth is out of the water. Instead, you should be exhaling out of your nose and mouth while your face is in the water (i.e., entering and exiting). Also, watch out for pressing the arm (opposite to the breathing side) down while breathing. The arm should stay extended while in the breathing position to create lift and stability rather than pressing down, which creates drag.

Best drill fix—One-arm drill with a kickboard, Superman catch-up.

More fluid swimming—Common issues include not feeling or engaging with the water or sending it in the wrong direction. Sometimes people are trying so hard, that they forget that they are working with water, need to be fluid, and aware of where they are sending the water. See Newton's Second Law!

Best drill fix—Practice "feeling" drills like treading water, sculling, and doggy paddle. Start with treading water so you can "feel" the water. Increase effort to feel more pressure and resistance. Proceed to sculling (in extended arm position, as well as pull phase) and doggie paddle. Feel the pressure on the water and yourself moving forward by directing the water backwards (Newton's Third Law).

Friday sets—You'll notice Fridays list "off" or swim. If you want to keep Friday off, you can switch your swim set to another day. Here are the three swim sets we'll use:

Set 1

WU:

» 200 mix of strokes and drills

MS:

» 3 x 100 descend (30")

» 50 easy

» 3 x 100 descend (30")

» 50 easy

» 1 x 100 fastest of workout (time)

CD:

» 200 easy swim

Total—1200

Set 2

WU:

» 300 mix of strokes and drills

MS:

» 4 x 50 build (30")

» 50 easy

» 3 x 100 descend (30")

» 50 easy

CD:

» 200 easy swim

Total—1100

Set 3

WU:

» 300 mix of strokes and drills

» 4 x 50 as 25 drill/25 swim (30")

MS:

» 4 x 50 build (30")

» 50 easy

» 8 x 25 Sprint (30")

» 50 easy

CD:

» 200 easy swim

Total—1200

THE BIKE

The midweek bike can be a spin or class at a cycling studio. The long bike on the weekend is one of your important workouts and should not be skipped. If you can find a place to get in a third weekly ride, it's highly recommended.

Effort levels—Your cycling warm-up and cool-down should always be easy (1 out of 5 on our RPE scale). It's expected that your midweek bike will include efforts of 4 to 5. Your weekend long rides should include a mix of RPE levels and average in the range of 1 to 3.

THE RUN

Run training is listed as run–walk in this plan. If you've already been running continuously, then switch the run–walk intervals to run, if desired. If you haven't been running at all, consider using the walk to run 5K plan that follows before you begin this plan.

Effort levels—Unless otherwise indicated, your walking warm-up and cool-down should always be easy (1 to 2 on our RPE scale). Unless otherwise indicated, your main set effort level should be moderate (3 out of 5 on our RPE scale). If running in general is a 4 or 5 out of 5 effort right now, don't worry about it! Running should become easier as your fitness progresses.

BEGINNER TRIATHLON PLAN

WEEK 10

	Monday	Tuesday	Wednesday	Thursday	Thursday	Friday	Saturday	Sunday
WU	WU: 100 yards easy swimming, 4 x 50 as 25 drill/25 swim	WU: 5 minutes easy walking	60 minutes outdoor cycling, indoor cycling, or spin class	WU: 5 minutes easy walking	WU: 100 yards easy swimming, 4 x 50 as 25 drill/25 swim	OFF or Swim set 1	10 miles cycling, easy to moderate	WU: 5 minutes easy walking
MS	MS: 3 x 100 with 30-second rest between each	MS: 8 (2' run/1' walk)		MS: 2 (8' run/2' walk)	MS: 5 minutes continuous swim			MS: 4 x .5-mile run with 1-minute walk break in between each
CD	CD: 100 easy	CD: 5 minutes walking		CD: 5 minutes walking	CD: 100 easy			CD: 5 minutes walking
Total	Total: 600 yards	Total time: approx. 35 minutes		Total time: 30 minutes	Total: 5 minutes continuous			Total run distance: 2 miles

WEEK 9

	Monday	Tuesday	Wednesday	Thursday	Friday	Saturday	Sunday
WU	WU: 100 yards easy swimming, 4 x 50 as 25 drill/25 swim	WU: 5 minutes easy walking	60 minutes outdoor cycling, indoor cycling, or spin class	WU: 5 minutes easy walking	OFF or Swim set 2 — WU: 100 yards easy swimming, 4 x 50 as 25 drill/25 swim	15 miles cycling, easy to moderate	WU: 5 minutes easy walking
MS	MS: 5 x 100 descend with 30-second rest between each	MS: 8 (3' run/1' walk)		MS: 2 (10' run/2' walk)	MS: 10 minutes continuous swim		MS: 1 x 1 miles run + 4 x /5 miles with 1-minute walk break in between each
CD	CD: 100 easy	CD: 5 minutes walking		CD: 6 minutes walking	CD: 100 easy		CD: 5 minutes walking
Total	Total: 800 yards	Total time: approx. 35 minutes		Total time: 35 minutes	Total: 5 minutes continuous		Total run distance: 3 miles

WEEK 8

	Monday	Tuesday	Wednesday	Thursday	Thursday	Friday	Saturday	Sunday
	WU: 100 yards easy swimming, 6 x 50 as 25 drill/25 swim	WU: 5 minutes easy walking	60 minutes outdoor cycling, indoor cycling, or spin class	WU: 5 minutes easy walking	WU: 100 yards easy swimming, 4 x 50 as 25 drill/25 swim	OFF or Swim set 3	20 miles cycling, easy to moderate followed by a 10-minute transition run	WU: 5 minutes easy walking
	MS: 4 x 150 with 30-second rest between each	MS: 8 (3' run/1' walk)		MS: 2 (14' run/2' walk)	MS: 15 minutes continuous swim			MS: 2 x 1 miles run + 3 x .5 miles with 1-minute walk break in between each
	CD: 100 easy	CD: 3 minutes walking		CD" 3 minutes walking	CD: 100 easy			CD: 5 minutes walking
	Total: 1,000 yards	Total time: approx. 40 minutes		Total time: 40 minutes	Total: 5 minutes continuous			Total run distance: 3.5 miles

WEEK 7

	Monday	Tuesday	Wednesday	Thursday	Friday	Saturday	Sunday
	WU: 100 yards easy swimming, 6 x 50 as 25 drill/25 swim	WU: 5 minutes easy walking	60 minutes outdoor cycling, indoor cycling, or spin class	OFF WU: 100 yards easy swimming, 4 x 50 as 25 drill/25 swim	OFF or Swim set 1	10 miles cycling, easy to moderate followed by a 10-minute transition run	WU: 5 minutes easy walking
	MS: 6 x 100 with 30-second rest between each. Descend 1 – 3 and 4 – 6.	MS: 6 (3' run/30" walk)		MS: 5 minutes continuous swim			MS: 2 x 1 miles run with 1-minute walk break in between each
	CD: 100 easy	CD: 4 minutes walking		CD: 100 easy			CD: 5 minutes walking
	Total: 1100 yards	Total time: 30 minutes		Total: 5 minutes continuous			Total run distance: 2 miles

283

WEEK 6

	Monday	Tuesday	Wednesday	Thursday	Thursday	Friday	Saturday	Sunday
WU	WU: 200 yards easy swimming, 4 x 50 as 25 drill/25 swim	WU: 5 minutes easy walking	60 minutes outdoor cycling, indoor cycling, or spin class	WU: 5 minutes easy walking	WU: 100 yards swimming, 4 x 50 as 25 drill/25 swim	OFF or Swim set 2	20 miles cycling, easy to moderate followed by a 15-minute transition run	WU: 5 minutes easy walking
MS	MS: 3 x 100 moderate with 30-second rest + 2 x 200 moderate with 30-second rest	MS: 6 (4' run/1' walk)		MS: 2 (10' run/2' walk)	MS: 15 minutes continuous swim			MS: 4 x 1 mile run with 1-minute walk break in between each
CD	CD: 100 easy	CD: 5 minutes walking		CD: 6 minutes walking	CD: 100 easy			CD: 5 minutes walking
Total	Total: 1,200 yards	Total time: 40 minutes		Total time: 35 minutes	Total: 15 minutes continuous			Total run distance: 4 miles

WEEK 5

	Monday	Tuesday	Wednesday	Thursday	Thursday	Friday	Saturday	Sunday
WU	WU: 200 yards easy swimming, 6 x 50 as 25 drill/25 swim	WU: 5 minutes easy walking	60 minutes outdoor cycling, indoor cycling, or spin class	WU: 4 minutes easy walking	WU: 100 yards easy swimming, 4 x 50 as 25 drill/25 swim	OFF or Swim set 3	25 miles cycling, easy to moderate followed by a 20-minute transition run	WU: 5 minutes easy walking
MS	MS: 3 x 200 with 30-second rest + 2 x 100 with 30-second rest	MS: 8 (4' run/30" walk)		MS: 3 (10' run/1' walk)	MS: 20 minutes continuous swim			MS: 2 (2 miles run) + 1 mile run with optional one-minute walk break in between each
CD	CD: 100 easy	CD: 4 minutes walking		CD: 3 minutes walking	CD: 100 easy			CD: 5 minutes walking
Total	Total: 1,400 yards	Total time: 45 minutes		Total time: 40 minutes	Total: 20 minutes continuous			Total run distance: 5 miles

COURAGE TO TRI

WEEK 4

Monday	Tuesday	Wednesday	Thursday	Friday	Saturday	Sunday
WU: 100 yards easy swimming, 4 x 50 as 25 drill/25 swim	WU: 5 minutes easy walking	60 minutes outdoor cycling, indoor cycling, or spin class	OFF	WU: 100 yards easy swimming, 4 x 50 as 25 drill/25 swim	OFF or Swim set 1	15 miles cycling, easy to moderate followed by a 10-minute transition run	WU: 5 minutes easy walking
MS: 2 x 200 with 30-second rest + 2 x 300 with 30-second rest	MS: 6 (4' run/30" walk)			MS: 25 minutes continuous swim			MS: 3 miles run continuous
CD: 100 easy	CD: 3 minutes walking			CD: 100 easy			CD: 5 minutes walking
Total: 1,400 yards	Total time: 35 minutes			Total: 25 minutes continuous			Total run distance: 3 miles

286

WEEK 3

Monday	Tuesday	Wednesday	Thursday	Thursday	Friday	Saturday	Sunday
WU: 100 yards easy swimming, 6 x 50 as 25 drill/25 swim	WU: 5 minutes easy walking	60 minutes outdoor cycling, indoor cycling, or spin class	WU: 6 minutes easy walking	WU: 100 yards easy swimming, 4 x 50 as 25 drill/25 swim	OFF or Swim set 2	25-30 miles cycling, easy to moderate followed by a 25-minute transition run	WU: 5 minutes easy walking
MS: 4 x 250 with 30-second rest between each	MS: 6 (5' run/1' walk)		MS: 3 (12' run/1' walk)	MS: 30 minutes continuous swim			MS: 2 x 2.5 miles run continuous with optional walk break between each
CD: 100 easy	CD: 4 minutes walking		CD: 5 minutes walking	CD: 100 easy			CD: 5 minutes walking
Total: 1,500 yards	Total time: 45 minutes		Total time: 50 minutes	Total: 30 minutes continuous			Total run distance: 5 miles

WEEK 2

	Monday	Tuesday	Wednesday	Thursday	Friday	Saturday	Sunday
WU	100 yards easy swimming, 4 x 50 as 25 drill/25 swim	5 minutes easy walking	60 minutes outdoor cycling, indoor cycling, or spin class	4 minutes easy walking; 100 yards easy swimming, 4 x 50 as 25 drill/25 swim	OFF or Swim set 3	12 miles cycling, easy to moderate	5 minutes easy walking
MS	3 x 400 with 30-second rest between each	4 (5' run/30" walk)		2 (15' run/1' walk); 15 minutes continuous swim			3 miles run continuous
CD	100 easy	3 minutes walking		4 minutes walking; 100 easy			5 minutes walking
Total	Total: 1,600 yards	Total time: 30 minutes		Total time: 40 minutes; Total: 15 minutes continuous			Total run distance: 3 miles

WEEK 1

Monday	Tuesday	Wednesday	Thursday	Friday	Saturday	Sunday
WU: 100 yards easy swimming, 4 x 50 as 25 drill/25 swim	WU: 4 minutes easy walking	60 minutes outdoor cycling, indoor cycling, or spin class	WU: 100 yards easy swimming, 4 x 50 as 25 drill/25 swim	OFF	20 minutes cycling, easy to moderate; do just enough to check gears on bike and make sure everything is working perfectly; .5-10 minutes transition on run	RACE DAY
MS: 3 x 100 with 30-second rest between each	MS: 3 (5' run/1' walk)		MS: 5 minutes continuous swim			
CD: 100 easy	CD: 3 minutes walking		CD: 100 easy			
Total: 600 yards	Total time: 25 minutes		Total: 5 minutes continuous			

BEGINNER WALK TO RUN 5K PLAN

WEEK 8

Day 1	Day 2	Day 3
WU: 5 minutes easy walking	WU: 5 minutes easy walking	WU: 5 minutes easy walking
MS: 10 (60" run/60" walk)	MS: 6 (30" run/60" walk)	MS: 4 x .25-mile run with 1-minute walk break between each
CD: 5 minutes walking	CD: 6 minutes walking	CD: 5 minutes walking
Total time: 30 minutes	**Total time: 20 minutes**	**Total run distance: 1 mile**

WEEK 7

Day 1	Day 2	Day 3
WU: 5 minutes easy walking	WU: 5 minutes easy walking	WU: 5 minutes easy walking
MS: 10 (60" run/60" walk)	MS: 8 (30" run/60" walk)	MS: 1 x .5-mile run + 4 x .25-mile with 1-minute walk break between each
CD: 5 minutes walking	CD: 3 minutes walking	CD: 5 minutes walking
Total time: 30 minutes	**Total time: 20 minutes**	**Total run distance: 1.5 miles**

WEEK 6

Day 1	Day 2	Day 3
WU: 5 minutes easy walking	WU: 5 minutes easy walking	WU: 5 minutes easy walking
MS: 10 (90" run/60" walk)	MS: 6 (60" run/60" walk)	MS: 2 x .5-mile run + 4 x .25-mile run with 1-minute walk break between each
CD: 5 minutes walking	CD: 3 minutes walking	CD: 5 minutes walking
Total time: 35 minutes	**Total time: 20 minutes**	**Total run distance: 2 miles**

WEEK 5

Day 1	Day 2	Day 3
WU: 5 minutes easy walking	WU: 5 minutes easy walking	WU: 5 minutes easy walking
MS: 8 (120" run/60" walk)	MS: 8 (60" run/60" walk)	MS: 1 x 1-mile run + 2 x .5-mile run + 2 x .25-mile run with 1-minute walk break between each
CD: 6 minutes walking	CD: 3 minutes walking	CD: 5 minutes walking
Total time: 35 minutes	**Total time: 20 minutes**	**Total run distance: 2.5 miles**

COURAGE TO TRI

WEEK 4

Day 1	Day 2	Day 3
WU: 5 minutes easy walking	WU: 5 minutes easy walking	WU: 5 minutes easy walking
MS: 8 (120" run/60" walk)	MS: 6 (90" run/60" walk)	MS: 2 x 1-mile run + 2 x .5-mile run with OPTIONAL 1-minute walk break between each
CD: 6 minutes walking	CD: 5 minutes walking	CD: 5 minutes walking
Total time: 35 minutes	**Total time: 25 minutes**	**Total run distance: 3 miles**

WEEK 3

Day 1	Day 2	Day 3
WU: 5 minutes easy walking	WU: 5 minutes easy walking	WU: 5 minutes easy walking
MS: 6 (3' run/1' walk)	MS: 8 (90" run/60" walk)	MS: 3 x 1-mile run with OPTIONAL 1-minute walk break between each
CD: 6 minutes walking	CD: 5 minutes walking	CD: 5 minutes walking
Total time: 35 minutes	**Total time: 30 minutes**	**Total run distance: 3 miles**

WEEK 2

Day 1	Day 2	Day 3
WU: 5 minutes easy walking	WU: 5 minutes easy walking	WU: 5 minutes easy walking
MS: 6 (3' run/1' walk)	MS: 6 (90" run/60" walk)	MS: 2-mile run with OPTIONAL 1-minute walk break between each
CD: 6 minutes walking	CD: 5 minutes walking	CD: 5 minutes walking
Total time: 35 minutes	**Total time: 25 minutes**	**Total run distance: 2 miles**

WEEK 1

Day 1	Day 2	Day 3
WU: 5 minutes easy walking	WU: 5 minutes easy walking	WU: 5 minutes easy
MS: 4(3' run/1' walk)	MS: 4(90" run/60" walk)	MS: 5K continuous
CD: 4 minutes walking	CD: 5 minutes walking	CD: 5 minutes walking
Total time: 25 minutes	**Total time: 20 minutes**	**Total run distance: 5K**

CREDITS

Design & Layout

Cover Design: Annika Naas

Interior Design: Anja Elsen

Layout: ZeroSoft

Photos

Cover Photo: © Bethany Rutledge

Interior Photos: All photos © Bethany Rutledge, unless otherwise noted

Editorial

Managing Editor: Elizabeth Evans